The Young Children's Encyclopedia

Volume 2

©1985 by Encyclopædia Britannica, Inc. Copyright under International Copyright Union.

All rights reserved under Pan American and Universal Copyright Conventions by Encyclopædia Britannica, Inc.

Printed in the U.S.A.
Library of Congress Catalog Card Number: 84-82313
International Standard Book Number: 0-85229-426-3

No part of this work may be reproduced or utilized in any form or by any means, electronic or mechanical, including photocopying, recording, or by any information storage and retrieval system without permission in writing from the publisher.

Encyclopædia Britannica, Inc.

Chicago
Auckland   Rome
Geneva   Seoul
London   Sydney
Manila   Tokyo
Paris   Toronto

Table of Contents   Volume 2

BABIES Baby's First Year, *pages 6-13*

Biggest Family, *pages 14-19*
*Can you imagine seeing a million fish eggs
. . . or more than a million hamsters?
Have you ever heard of such big families?*

BACH, JOHANN SEBASTIAN The Boy Who Loved Music, *pages 20-21*

BALLET So Much to Remember, *pages 22-27*

More About Ballet, *pages 28-29*

BALLOONS All Kinds of Balloons, *pages 30-35*
*Guess what took the very first ride in a
balloon. A duck, a rooster, and a sheep!
Today you can ride in a giant balloon
if you want to!*

BAMBOO The Tallest Grass, *pages 36-39*

BANANAS Jungle Gold, *pages 40-43*
*What grows upside down and looks as if
it has 15 "hands" and 20 "fingers"?*

BANKS And This Little Piggy Went to the Bank,
pages 44-49
*A piggy bank filled with pennies is taken
on a mysterious trip to a big bank downtown.*

BANNEKER, BENJAMIN The Man Who Remembered, *pages 50-51*

BARNUM, PHINEAS TAYLOR Come See the Humbug—25¢, *pages 52-53*
*A lady who looked like a fish . . . another
lady with a beard . . . clowns and giants . . .
Phineas T. Barnum and his exciting circus!*

BASEBALL How Pitchers Fool Batters, *pages 54-55*

BATS It Flies, but It's Not a Bird, *pages 56-59*
*Have you ever seen a flying furry animal
that hangs upside down in dark places,
sleeps all day, and guides itself by special
echoes? If you have, you've seen a bat!*

BEACH   Sand Castles, *pages 60-63*
You build a sand castle with walls and towers and secret tunnels . . . will a wave come and knock it down?

More About the Beach, *pages 64-65*

BEARS   Watch Out for Bears!, *pages 66-69*

BEAVERS   The Busy Animal, *pages 70-73*
Beavers build wonderful houses all by themselves . . . they're the busiest animals of all.

BEES   A Hive Is a House for Bees, *pages 74-79*
What would you see if you looked inside a beehive? Hundreds of bees in tiny six-sided rooms doing special jobs, such as building, housekeeping, and guarding the hive.

Honeybee at Work, *pages 80-85*
Did you know that the big red apples that you eat couldn't have grown without the help of bees?

BEETHOVEN, LUDWIG VAN   The Lonely Giant, *pages 86-87*

BELL, ALEXANDER GRAHAM   The First Telephone, *pages 88-89*
A little wooden box buzzes and hums . . . suddenly words come out of the box . . . the telephone has been invented!

More About Alexander Graham Bell, *pages 90-91*

BELLS   Ding-Dong Bell, *pages 92-95*

BIRDS   What Is a Bird?, *pages 96-99*
Some birds don't *fly . . . some creatures have wings and* aren't *birds . . . just what makes a bird a bird?*

Welcome, Birds, *pages 100-101*

A Good Day for Robins, *pages 102-107*

The Boy Who Hated Cages, *pages 108-111*

BLACKWELL, ELIZABETH   The First Woman Doctor, *pages 112-113*
The first woman in the U.S. to become a doctor had to go through many hardships to earn her title.

BOLÍVAR, SIMÓN   Hero of Many Nations, *pages 114-115*
One man leads a small army over snowcapped mountains and across flooded plains to free many people in South America.

BOOKS   Who's in the Library?, *pages 116-117*
A first adventure in reading.

Tim Says, *pages 118-119*

More About Books, *pages 120-121*

BOONE, DANIEL   How Daniel Boone Learned from Nature, *pages 122-123*
He learned from raccoons how to climb trees . . . from otters how to swim . . . from owls how to hoot!

BREAD   Fresh from the Bakery, *pages 124-127*

BRIDGES   Roads in the Air, *pages 128-133*

BRONTE SISTERS   Three Famous Sisters, *pages 134-135*

BRONTOSAUR   The Big, Big Ones, *pages 136-137*

BUBBLES   A Thousand Balloons in One Afternoon, *pages 138-139*

BUCKINGHAM PALACE   A Famous Royal Home, *pages 140–141*

BUFFALO   King of the American Beasts, *pages 142-145*

BUGS   What Kind of Bug Is This?, *pages 146-149*

BUILDINGS   People Who Work Up High, *pages 150-153*
Special giant-sized machines . . . hundreds of shiny windows . . . it's fun to watch men build skyscrapers!

BUNYAN, PAUL   A Very Special Lumberjack, *pages 154-155*

BUTTONS   Holding Clothes Together, *pages 156-159*

Here are more words beginning with "B" ... *and* ... Here is where you may read about them

Baboon	Monkeys, *Book 10, page 96*
Bagpipe	Music, *Book 10, page 158*
Ballot	Elections, *Book 5, page 68*
Banyan tree	Trees, *Book 15, page 110*
Bastille	Liberty, *Book 9, page 62*
Battery	Electricity, *Book 5, page 72*
	Flashlight, *Book 6, page 76*
Beetle	Nature, *Book 11, page 30*
Bison	Buffalo, *Book 2, page 142*
Blindness	Eyes and Ears, *Book 5, page 156*
Body	You, *Book 16, pages 136 to 151*
Bomb	Dynamite, *Book 4, page 158*
Bone	You, *Book 16, page 144*
Braille	Eyes and Ears, *Book 5, page 152*
Brain	You, *Book 16, page 148*
Brazil	Rio de Janeiro, *Book 13, page 110*
Bronco	Ranching, *Book 13, page 52*
Bull	Farming, *Book 6, page 46*
Burbank, Luther	Plants, *Book 12, page 106*
Butterfly	Directions, *Book 4, page 54*
	Insects, *Book 8, page 48*
Byrd, Richard	Exploring, *Book 5, page 118*

BABIES

Baby's First Year

My little brother, who just came,
Hasn't even got a name!
Look at his fingernails! So small
You hardly notice them at all.
Perhaps someday he'll learn to walk!
Perhaps someday he'll learn to talk!
But *now* all he can do is yell
And *that* he does *extremely* well.
Today my mommy said, "Once *you*
Were just like him."—And if that's true,
The chances are someday he'll be
A real live *person*—just like me.

On the day it's born, a baby bear could fit into your two hands. It's that tiny.

But by the time it's one year old, a bear cub is almost as big as the mother bear. It'll soon be ready to move out of the den that has been its home. It has learned the ways of grown-up bears.

By the time a cat or a dog is one year old, it's grown-up, too.

The very day it's born, a little colt can stand on its own legs. They're wobbly legs, and sometimes it tumbles—*oops!* But soon it knows all about walking.

The day *you* were born you couldn't do much except eat and sleep and cry. You couldn't even turn around by yourself.

You were bigger than a new bear cub, but you grew much more slowly.

For many years after they're born, children need to be taken care of by their mother and father.

At first, a baby can't move the way he really wants to. He kicks his feet and waves his hands in the air. But he can't do these things *on purpose*.

His head wobbles when he lifts it and then drops right down again. Months go by before the new baby is strong enough to hold up his head and look around. *Then* is he surprised!

It's a long time before baby starts reaching for things. At first he can only grab at something he wants to pick up or slap at it or play with it, much the way a kitten paws at a ball of yarn. But later baby discovers that he has *thumbs* as well as fingers and that he can pick up and hold things between his fingers and thumb.

Thumbs are very important to have. Try to pick up a pin, a ball, or a piece of string without using your thumb. Aren't you glad that your thumb is so handy—and that your hand is so thumby?

After learning what a fine thing a thumb is, each time baby touches Mommy's hair or Daddy's tie—or nose—he opens his fingers wide, closes them tight, and hangs on.

All this time baby is getting ready to walk. He wiggles and squirms, and then one day he rolls right over. *Waagh!* He may howl with rage and surprise the first time that happens. Soon, though, baby likes his new trick. And he likes the next one even better—being able to sit up without being held.

Then one day baby gets up on his hands and knees—and suddenly he's crawling! Now he can go from the chair to the table to the bookcase and can even pull himself up to stand. About the time he has his first birthday, he forgets to hang on to Mommy's hand and takes his first step alone.

Now baby can walk. He toddles and waddles from the kitchen to the bedroom to the front door. Sometimes he even tries to run. That's when he gets into trouble. It seems that he will never learn. But he's learning all the time. He just doesn't know he's learning. He finds out that chairs turn over, that dishes break, and that books can fall on his head.

Sometimes we call it mischief—but baby is just busy exploring. He moves, looks, and touches. He's like a puppy dog, poking and roaming and sniffing.

By now, baby is learning something else just as important as walking or using his thumbs and fingers. He is learning to *talk*.

All during his first year, baby has been making gurgles and chuckles and easy sounds like *da-da-da* or *ma-ma-ma*. His family is so happy when he says Mama that he says it again and again. He can understand some of the things his parents or brothers and sisters say to him now, especially no, no. He learns to say them, too.

By this time, a kitten has grown into a cat and probably has even had her own kittens. The young bear has learned to find its own food and can protect itself well enough to live alone. Baby can't do that. Not yet. He still has much growing and learning and exploring to do.

Can you remember when *you* learned to walk?

If you liked this article, read Age *in Volume 1.*

WALKING

I *think* I can remember back
   To when I couldn't walk at all,
And, just to get from here to there,
   I had to crawl and *crawl* and CRAWL.

The chairs, the chest of drawers, the desk
   All used to seem so far away!
They wouldn't even stir when I
   Invited them to come and play.

But then one day I took a step
   And then I took another one.
I learned to walk—and even more:
   To skip and hop and jump and run!

BABIES

Biggest Family

A mother fish lays more eggs than you can count—often more than a million. She doesn't stay to take care of the baby fish that come from the eggs. After she drops her eggs in the water, she swims away.

When a baby fish comes out of one of the eggs, it has *hatched*. But not many of the eggs do hatch. Other fish—and frogs and turtles—eat many of the fish eggs. Some of the eggs float onto the land, where birds eat them.

A mother bird usually lays only as many eggs as can be kept warm with her body—usually four or five eggs. After they're hatched, she feeds and protects the baby birds and helps them learn to fly.

Very large animals, such as horses and cows and elephants, almost always have only one baby at a time.

But small animals, such as mice and rabbits and opossums, have several babies at a time.

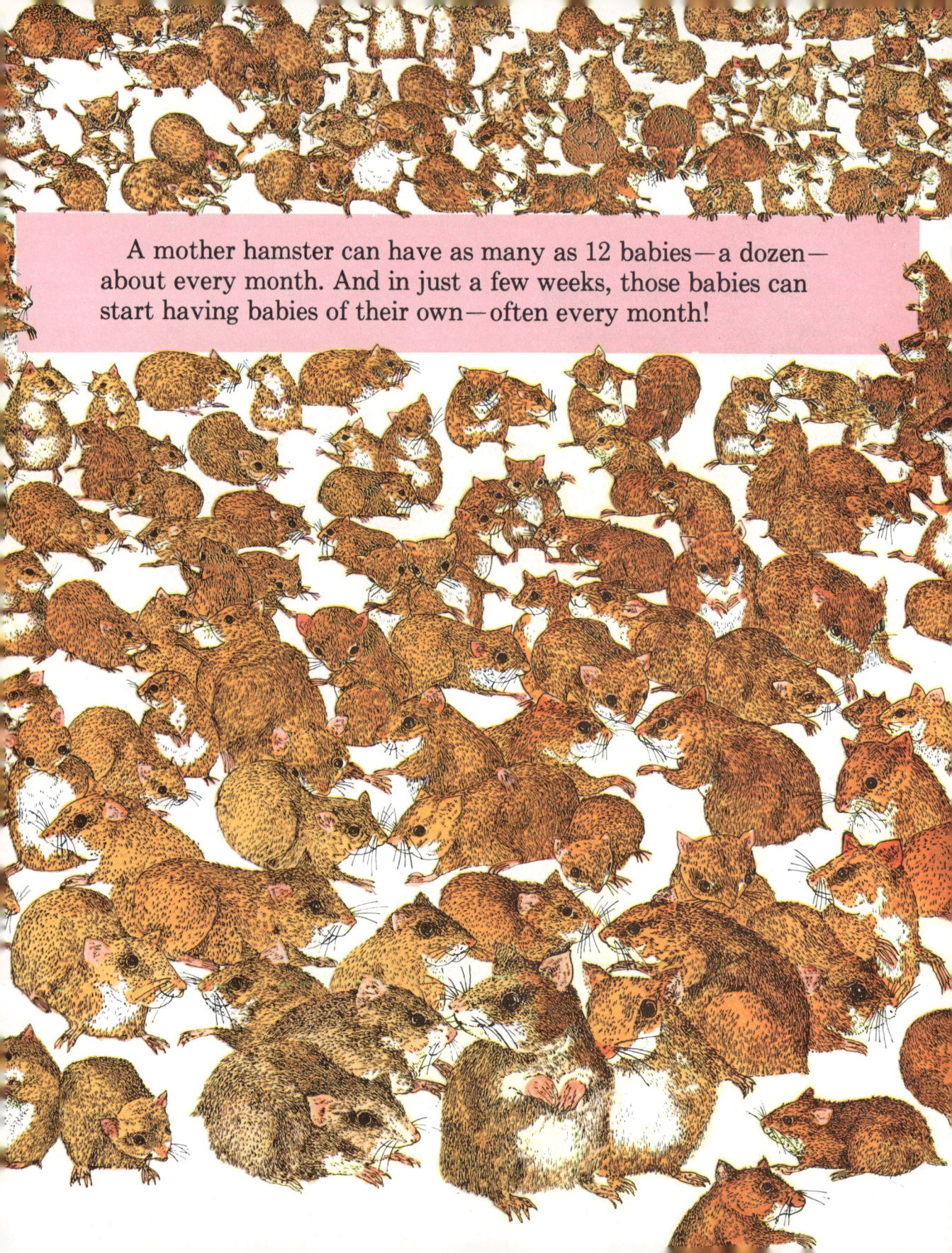

A mother hamster can have as many as 12 babies—a dozen—about every month. And in just a few weeks, those babies can start having babies of their own—often every month!

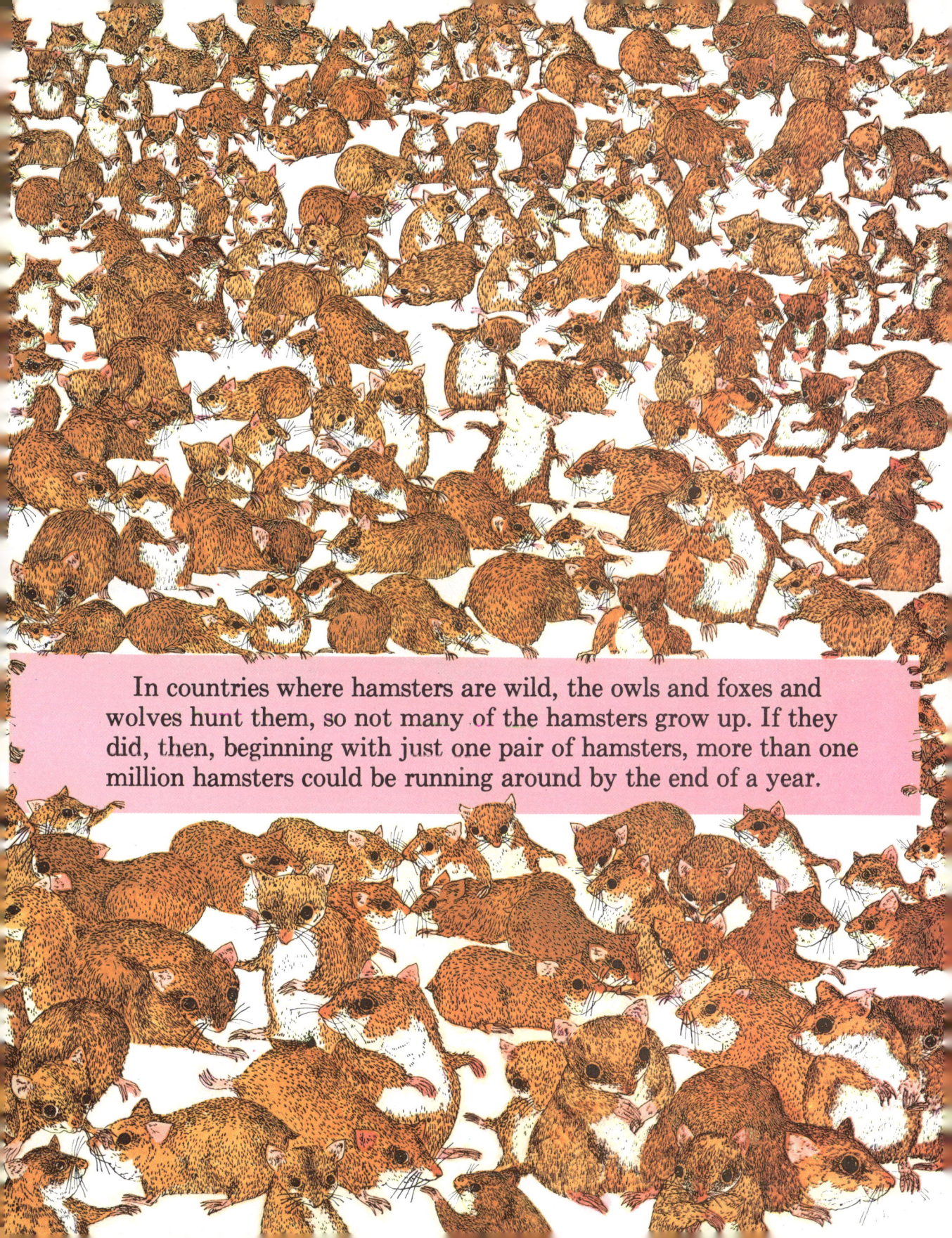

In countries where hamsters are wild, the owls and foxes and wolves hunt them, so not many of the hamsters grow up. If they did, then, beginning with just one pair of hamsters, more than one million hamsters could be running around by the end of a year.

Boys and girls are almost always born one at a time.

When they're born two at a time, they're called *twins*.

When they're born three at a time, they're called *triplets*.

When they're born four at a time, they're called *quadruplets*.

Once in a great, great while they're born five at a time, and then they're called *quintuplets*.

Babies grow slowly, and they grow for a long time. And during all this time their parents take care of them and keep them safe and try to help them grow up happily.

It takes a long time before a human family can grow this big.

BACH, JOHANN SEBASTIAN

The Boy Who Loved Music

Music filled the house whenever the Bach family got together. Many people in the family were musicians, and some of them were hired to play for princes, dukes, and other noblemen. Music was part of almost everyone's life, especially in Germany, where Johann Sebastian Bach was born.

Johann Sebastian was about seven years old when he began to learn to read music. Soon he was playing the violin and viola and singing with a special church group.

He once spent many nights copying organ music. He had to do this by moonlight when everyone else was sleeping, because he wasn't supposed to touch the special book of music he was copying from. Yet the music was more important to him than the scolding he knew he would get if he were found out.

When he went away to school, he spent his vacations walking many miles to hear organists play. Before long he himself was to become a famous writer of music and a great organist.

Bach sometimes got into trouble when he played church music in unusual ways. But he wouldn't apologize when he shocked the church people with extra trills and frills. He was playing the music the way he thought it should sound.

One time, when working for a duke, Bach decided to leave and go to work for a prince. The duke was furious and had Bach arrested. Bach spent his time in the guardhouse, or jail, writing more music for the organ.

Although more than 200 years have passed since Bach died, he is still considered one of the four or five greatest composers who ever lived.

Other stories about famous composers can be found under Mozart *in Volume 10 and* Stravinsky *in Volume 14.*

BALLET

So Much to Remember

"Anita, we're waiting," said Miss Margot.

Anita went over to the bar, stood up tall, put her heels together, and turned her feet out as far as she could.

"That's first position," said Miss Margot. "I want third position. Third position."

Anita kept her toes turned out but slid one foot alongside the other. Miss Margot started the record player.

"Now," she said, "*demi-plié*, and one . . . two . . . three, and. . . ."

Anita and the other girls bent their knees while Miss Margot counted in time to the music. They moved up and down very smoothly and slowly, as if they were practicing sitting down.

Anita liked to hear Miss Margot use the French words to tell them what to do. Miss Margot had told them that French was the language used in ballet because the first great ballet school was in France.

Anita knew that *demi-plié* meant to bend her knees but only halfway (*demi* means "half" in French) so that she could keep her heels on the floor.

"Heels on the floor, Roselin," said Miss Margot.

"Roselin did a *plié* instead of a *demi-plié*," Anita thought. "*Plié* means bending your knees all the way so that you can't keep your heels on the floor." Anita was glad that she had not made that mistake.

But while Anita was feeling good about that, Miss Margot said, "Open your fingers, Anita. Lift your arm higher and reach."

"So many things to think about!" Anita thought as she lifted her arm higher and opened her fist.

After class Anita put on her street clothes and waited for her mother to come and drive her home.

"You're doing very well," Miss Margot said.

"It's hard to keep my balance," Anita said, "and to remember everything all the time."

"You just have to keep practicing," Miss Margot said, smiling.

"I know," said Anita. But she didn't really know. She didn't believe that she would ever remember *or* learn to keep her balance or anything else.

That night after supper she told her mother, "I've been taking ballet lessons for months and months, and I still can't dance very well. Miss Margot has to correct me all the time."

"That's her job," her mother said. "She's the teacher."

"Anyway, I'd like to stop for a while—after the recital next week—if that's all right."

"If that's what you really want, you may. But I'd think about it carefully. Lots of things are hard at first, when you're just learning, but they get easier."

Anita's friend Sally was taking violin lessons. Anita thought she might like to try the violin. She was glad when the last ballet class was finished.

"Tomorrow evening we'll have a dress rehearsal," Miss Margot said. "Bring your costumes, and everybody please be on time. All of my other classes will be there, too."

When Anita got to the rehearsal the next night, she was surprised to see so many girls there. The costumes were beautiful, and many of them were decorated with tiny, sparkling circles called *sequins*.

Anita's class was one of the first to dance. It seemed strange not to have Miss Margot shouting, "Anita, chin up. Anita, point! Point your toe! *Adagio! Adagio!*"

And then the oldest class came on, running lightly on the tips of their toes, whirling gracefully, leaping, and then running again. Anita's eyes opened wide and she held her breath as one of the turning girls lifted her leg straight out behind her, with toe pointed and arms held out gracefully.

She turned smoothly, with chin held high and eyes looking straight ahead. As she turned, she looked straight at Anita, standing in the wings. Anita couldn't believe how beautifully the girl danced—leaping, spinning, never losing her balance.

When the dance was over, Miss Margot said, "Very nice, Marie. But arch just a little more on the *arabesque*."

"So that's her name," Anita thought. "Marie!" And then without thinking about it, she said it again, out loud, "Marie!" Some of the girls looked at Anita, who then felt embarrassed.

"Set up for the next number," Miss Margot said.

Anita felt someone touch her shoulder.

"Did you call me?" Marie asked, smiling down at her.

Anita didn't know what to say. She felt terrible. "I'm just Anita," she said finally. "I can't dance very well."

Marie laughed and leaned down beside the little ballerina. "Of course you can," she said. "I saw you. You were second from the end, in the second row."

"But I lose my balance, and sometimes I forget to hold my chin up or——"

"I used to lose my balance and forget, too," said Marie. "I still do some of the time."

"Really?" asked Anita.

"Honestly," Marie answered, taking Anita's hand. "When I first started, Miss Margot corrected me more than anyone else in my whole class."

The next night on the way to the recital, Anita said to her mother, "Watch for my friend Marie. You can tell who she is because she's the best ballet dancer in the whole recital. And if I keep practicing, some day soon I'm going to dance almost as well as she does."

BALLET

More About Ballet

"Dance me a story."

You might think it sounds funny to ask someone to dance a story for you, but that is what ballet dancers do.

The story that a ballet tells may have been made up many years before. Some ballets tell the stories of old fairy tales. *Cinderella* and *The Sleeping Beauty* are just two of the children's fairy tales that have been made into ballets.

If you already have read either of these stories or have seen them as plays, you might like to see how these stories can be told by using only music and dancing and no words at all.

The kind of music that a *composer* writes for a ballet depends on the story. When Cinderella is dancing happily with the Prince, the music is light and happy.

But when she sits alone by the fireplace, the music is so slow and sad that it makes you feel sad.

The man who makes up the dances—the *choreographer*—listens to the music while he decides which steps the ballet dancer will use. These steps must suit the music, as well as help tell the story.

When the story is happy, he chooses many leaps and turns—happy tip-of-the-toes dancing for the ballerinas and high leaps for the man. (Toe dancers wear special shoes that make it possible for them to dance on the tips of their toes.)

When Cinderella is sad, she still dances gracefully, but her steps may be slower and she may dance on the flat part of her foot, even though she is wearing toe shoes. She may lower her head and let her arms hang down like the limbs of a weeping willow tree.

When the Prince lifts Cinderella high into the air after he has put the slipper on her foot, it looks very easy. Actually it is very hard. The dancers have worked for many years to learn to make it look so easy.

Many modern ballets are more colorful and gay than the early ballets were. The dancers work harder to seem like the characters they are dancing. Some ballets are about everyday things—some mix usual dance steps with such common movements as walking down the street.

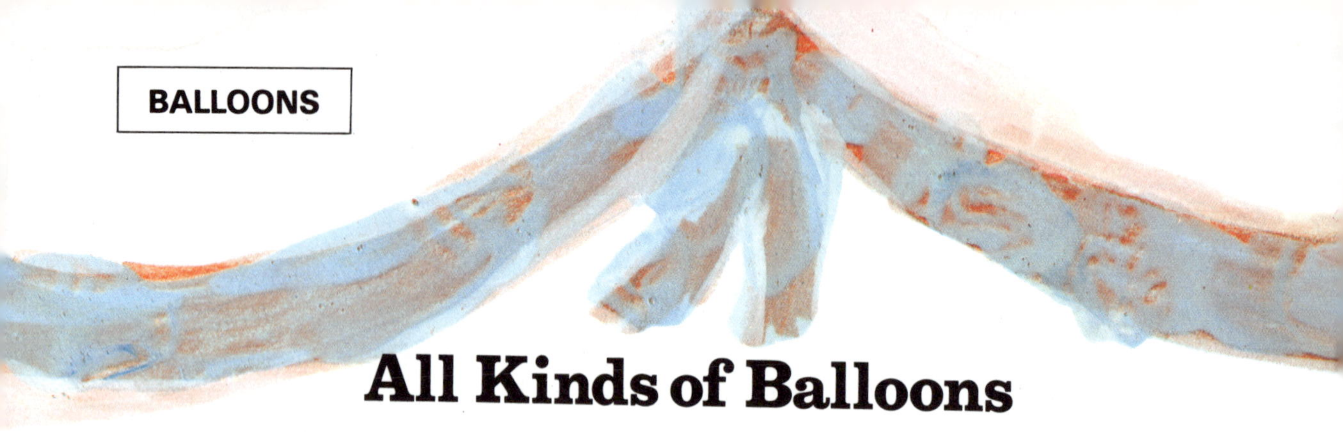

BALLOONS

All Kinds of Balloons

If you were going to have a birthday party, which balloon would you choose for your guests? This one or the one on the next page?

Both are red and made of rubber. Each is no bigger or smaller than the other. Then what is there to choose between?

This balloon won't go up unless it's tossed up, and it won't stay up unless you keep tapping it up.

This is a "come-right-down" balloon.

It can be blown up with air from your mouth. It's as light as a feather. You can toss and punch and catch and bounce it.

This balloon goes up all by itself, and it stays up unless you pull it back down. It will stand up by itself on the end of a string, as neat as a fresh flower on a stem.

This is a "stay-up" balloon.

This kind of balloon must be filled with something that isn't air but looks like air (which means that it doesn't look like anything at all).

If you let go of the string, the balloon floats away, high in the sky!

The balloon that rises is filled with a gas called *helium*. Helium is lighter than air. A balloon filled with helium weighs less than a similar balloon filled with air. Balloons filled with helium sail up in the air, high into the sky, unless you hold them down with a string.

A toy balloon is not the only kind that can float. Long before there were rockets or airplanes, giant balloons lifted people into the air.

A giant balloon sailed high over Paris, France, nearly 200 years ago. But there were no people in that balloon. The king of France wanted to find out whether people and animals could live high in the air. So the first to get a ride in the balloon were a duck, a rooster, and a sheep.

'Way above the rooftops, 'way above the steeple,
They looked far down at the king and his people.
The duck said, "Quack! We're bigger than the king!"
The rooster wouldn't stop his cock-a-doodle-dooing.
The woolly-headed sheep said, "Baa-baa-baa,"
While the teeny-weeny king cheered, "Rah, rah, rah!"

Afterwards people began taking rides high in the air in pretty balloons while people below watched and held their breath. They wondered whether the riders could get down alive.

When the men landed safely, people cheered and threw their hats into the air. They were so happy that they had a big celebration. There was dancing that day in the streets.

Later lots of people made balloons. Giant balloons went up carrying bands playing music and ballet dancers dancing. One balloon even lifted a performing white horse and its rider over a city.

Below, men moved through the crowds, selling toy balloons to children for souvenirs.

Even dresses for little girls and women were made to look like balloons.

But these wonderful old balloons weren't safe! In those days, people didn't have helium to put into a balloon. Instead, they built a fire under it to fill it with hot air. Since the hot air was lighter than the air around it, the balloon rose. But sometimes the fire burned the balloon. Sometimes it burned the grass around it and even the houses nearby.

The balloons stayed up only as long as the air inside them was hotter than the air outside. When the air in the balloon cooled off, the balloon came down—sometimes *kerplunk!*

Today balloons are safer. We don't have to light a fire and fill a balloon with hot air and smoke. We fill balloons with helium. It can lift any kind of balloon into the air—your little red balloon at a birthday party or a giant balloon that could carry you as high as the clouds.

Want to learn more?
Read about Kites *in Volume 8*
or about Liquids, Solids, and Gases *in Volume 9.*

BAMBOO

The Tallest Grass

Did you ever see grass growing high as a tree—a *tall* tree? Bamboo is this kind of grass.

It grows up straight and thin, with branches at the top. You could go twisting and squirming through a bamboo forest like a bug crawling through grass in the park.

But although bamboo is really a kind of grass, it looks more like a tree—a beautiful tree. It has long leaves that sway in the wind like slim fingers reaching to touch something. Japanese poets write poems and songs about bamboo, and artists paint it in pictures.

Not *all* bamboo grows tall. Altogether there are more than 500 different kinds of bamboo, and some grow no higher than your ankles. Bamboo grows best in places where it is warm and where it rains often. Some kinds of bamboo grow very fast—almost as much in one day as you are tall! If they are growing near a house, their slim leaves brush the roof gently and cool the house with their shade.

Some bloom and have seeds every year. Some never bloom at all. Some bloom only once, after living about 40 years, and then die. New shoots of bamboo come up from around the roots of the old ones.

But the most interesting thing about this remarkable plant is what people do with it after it is cut down. Bamboo probably has more uses than any other plant in the world.

Bamboo is not a tree, remember, so the long straight stems of bamboo are not like tree wood. They are hollow, which makes them very light. You could lift a big piece of bamboo with one hand. At the same time, bamboo is so strong that people use it to build houses, and even high bridges over rivers.

Many people, in countries where it's always warm, have houses made almost entirely of bamboo—the walls, the roof, the floor. Nearly everything inside their houses is made of bamboo, too. The chairs—tables—curtains—birdcages—cooking pots—flower vases—drinking cups. And the fence around their yard is made of bamboo.

Some bamboo is thinner than your little finger. Some is much thicker than your waist. And because it is hollow, it can be fitted together and used for pipes to carry water. Many farmers' fields are watered, or *irrigated,* by water brought from a river or lake through bamboo pipes.

When bamboo is used for building, it can be used just as it is, or it can be split into long thin strips and stuck together or tied together. But bamboo is used for more than building.

People eat it!

The tender young shoots of bamboo are crisp and tasty. Some are put into cans and shipped all over the world. You may have eaten bamboo shoots in a Chinese or a Japanese restaurant.

Cows eat the leaves of some kinds of bamboo.

Bamboo is also made into paper. The soft pulp inside the hard stems is taken out and sent to a factory. There it is made into a fine paper in just about the way wood pulp is made into paper.

And, as if that weren't enough, bamboo makes good walking sticks and fishing poles. And there's no telling what new use someone may find for this special kind of grass—bamboo.

Are you interested in Plants?
You may also read about them in Volume 12.

BANANAS

Jungle Gold

It has as many as 15 "hands."
Sometimes it has 20 "fingers" on each hand.
It looks as if it is growing upside down!
When it's one year old, it's as big as it will ever be.
What is it?
It's a *banana plant*.

The "hands" aren't real hands. They're the bunches of bananas that grow around the stem. The "fingers" are the bananas.

Bananas don't grow on trees. They grow on a thick stalk that looks just a little like a cornstalk. The stalk is soft enough to be cut with a knife.

It takes about a year before bananas are ready to be picked. Some are as small as fingers. Others are as long and as thick as a man's arm. Some banana plants grow as tall as a house—even taller!

Not all bananas are eaten as fruit. Some never get sweet, and they are cooked as a vegetable.

People in most countries never see a banana until it reaches the grocery store. But if you visited a country where it's hot and rains many days of every year, you might see a banana *plantation*, the large farm where bananas grow.

All the plants you see in this picture are banana plants, even though there are bananas on only one of them.

This good-tasting fruit doesn't come from a seed but from a root planted deep in the ground. First a stalk pushes up into the air. Then leaves appear. At the beginning the banana plant grows very fast—sometimes as much in one night as the length of your feet. Soon, sweet-smelling flowers bloom, and when their petals drop off, a cluster of bananas begins to grow.

As they get bigger, the bananas start turning up. It looks as if they're growing upside down!

Bananas are ready to eat when they turn soft and yellow. But they're picked long before this—when they're hard and bright green. This is because bananas have to travel many miles before they arrive at a grocery store. On trucks and boats and trains, bananas travel all over the world. There are special boats just for bananas, and special trains that keep them just cool enough so that they will get ripe while traveling. If bananas were picked when they were ripe, they would spoil on the way.

Most bananas are grown in South America.
You may want to look under Amazon *in Volume 1*
to learn about a part of this continent.

BANKS

And This Little Piggy Went to the Bank

On Danny Price's fourth birthday his grandmother gave him a piggy bank.

When Danny's father came home from work he said, "That's the biggest piggy bank I ever saw. He looks more like a pig than a piggy!"

"He has a big smile, too," said Danny. "I'm going to call him Smiley."

"Are you planning to feed him every day?" asked Danny's father.

"Yes," said Danny, looking very serious. "Grandma said that he needed to eat at least a penny a day. So I have to get some jobs."

"I have a job for you right now," said Danny's mother. "I'll give you a penny for Smiley's first meal if you take that wastebasket full of torn wrapping paper out to the big trash can."

Smiley slept with Danny that night. Each time Danny turned over and heard the penny rattling in Smiley's big stomach, Danny smiled in his sleep.

All winter long Smiley grew heavier and heavier—and no wonder! Danny fed him at least once a day. He could always count on a penny for emptying the wastebaskets for his mother. And he watered her houseplants every Tuesday and Thursday. She was proud of the way he never forgot. "He takes better care of them than I did," she told Danny's father.

Danny earned another penny a day by waking up his big brother so he'd get to work on time. Of course, his big brother had an alarm clock, but he had the habit of sleeping through its *r-r-r-r-r-ing*. So he hired Danny to come into his room, right after

the alarm had sounded, and turn on the light and stamp around.

The nice old lady across the hall gave Danny a penny for mailing her letters at the corner mailbox on cold, wet days when the sidewalks were slippery. At first Danny didn't want to take the penny. But the old lady said, "You have the fattest pig in the neighborhood. Now you *keep* him that way." She pressed the penny into Danny's hand.

Danny's father gave him five pennies a week for putting the morning paper back together after the rest of the family had read it. As Danny's father sat down each evening to read the newspaper stories that

he'd only had time to glance at in the morning, he would say, "I'm sure glad we've got Smiley!"

Danny was glad, too. His days were more exciting and full of things to do, now that he had Smiley to think about.

But one bright Saturday morning in late spring, Danny did not look glad at all. His father was having a second cup of coffee as Danny came into the kitchen.

"Smiley's sick," Danny said. "Smiley is very sick."

"Danny," said his mother, "you must remember Smiley is just a piggy bank. And piggy banks can't really get sick."

"Well, if he's not sick now, he's going to get sick," Danny said. "He won't eat. I tried to feed him a penny this morning, and he wouldn't take it."

"Let's have a look," said Danny's father.

Danny's father shook the heavy pig. "Just what I thought. He's eaten all the pennies he can hold."

"Do you think he'd eat a dime, maybe?" asked Danny eagerly. "Dimes are smaller than pennies."

Danny's father shook his head. "Smiley can't eat a thing until we shake all these pennies out of him."

Danny ran to the kitchen to look for a sack big enough to hold all Smiley's pennies. When he got back his father said, "I have a better idea. Let's take Smiley, pennies and all, to my savings bank. They have a machine over there that can count all those pennies in about a minute. And they'll keep the money safe for you."

"They won't keep Smiley, too, will they?"

"No, only what's inside Smiley."

The bank was quiet, even though there were lots of people in it. They seemed to speak more softly and walk more slowly than people did in other places. Danny looked around the enormous room. He liked the thick blue carpeting and the bright green potted plants, some of them taller than bushes in the park. The *flap-flap* of the revolving door caught his attention.

"Dad, look!" He pointed to the door. "None of those people have piggy banks. They're all leaving without them!"

"I'll bet they didn't come in with piggy banks either," said Danny's father. "They probably had salary checks or money."

His father led him over to one side of the bank where there was a high counter.

One of the men behind the counter smiled when he saw Danny's father and said, "Hello, Mr. Price."

"Mr. Lenz, I'd like you to meet my youngest son, Danny."

"And this is Smiley," said Danny, holding up the piggy bank.

"What a fine looking piggy bank," said Mr. Lenz. "He looks as if he'd be worth a lot of money."

"Oh no, he's not for sale! You can't have *him*," said Danny. "Just the *pennies* that are inside him."

"I know how you feel," said Mr. Lenz, "so we'll settle for the pennies." He pressed a button and a few moments later a young woman appeared. "This is Danny Price, our newest depositor," he told her, "and he's probably the youngest man to start saving his money at our bank."

Mr. Lenz turned to Danny and said, "Miss Taylor is going to take Smiley down to the service department where there's a machine that will count all those pennies." Mr. Lenz seemed to read Danny's thoughts. "And after they're counted, she'll bring Smiley right back."

When Miss Taylor returned and handed him a slip of paper, Mr. Lenz said, "You certainly know how to feed a piggy bank, Danny. You have ten dollars and seven cents."

Danny didn't smile until Miss Taylor put Smiley into his arms.

Mr. Lenz handed Danny a small flat book. "You keep this little book," he said. "It tells you how many pennies we're keeping for you. Anytime you want them back, you just come in and tell me. But remember, the longer you let us keep your money, the more it will grow."

"Money *grows?*" Danny looked at the tall plants and wondered how that could be.

"We pay you for letting us use your money. The longer we use it, the more we pay you."

As he walked with his father to the car, Danny fished a penny out of his coat pocket and dropped it into Smiley. "He's all well! I'm going to fill him up again and bring him back with another stomachful of pennies."

You may learn about Money *in Volume 10.*

BANNEKER, BENJAMIN

The Man Who Remembered

Benjamin Banneker was born a few months before another great American—George Washington. Benjamin was black, but he was not a slave. He and his mother and his grandmother were free.

Benjamin's grandmother came from England. In America she got a job and worked for many years to pay for her boat trip across the ocean. After working many more years, she saved enough money to buy a farm. Benjamin lived with her for a while. She taught him to read and write and do arithmetic.

Benjamin's neighbors knew that he was smart. They were not surprised when he built a large wooden clock. He made each piece after studying a small pocket watch. The clock made him famous, for it was one of the first clocks built in America. People from other colonies began to send puzzles of all kinds for Benjamin to solve.

Thomas Jefferson learned of Benjamin Banneker's ability to solve hard problems. He asked Banneker to help build the city that was to be our country's capital—Washington, D.C.

Banneker worked hard on the plans for the city. He marked where the streets and buildings—the Capitol, the White House, and many others—should be built.

Later, Major L'Enfant, the Frenchman who had designed the new city, had an argument and went back to France in anger. He took all of the plans with him. The workmen couldn't build without any plans to follow.

For a while it seemed that the plans for our capital might have to be changed. But Benjamin Banneker remembered the plans he had helped draw. He redrew each plan just as he once had built each piece of his clock.

If it weren't for Benjamin Banneker, our capital might look very different from the way it does today.

Read about Washington, D.C., *in Volume 16.*

BARNUM, PHINEAS TAYLOR

Come See the Humbug—25¢

"Step right up, folks. See the lady with the body of a fish." Humbug!

"And in this tent you will see an animal never seen before by man or beast. This animal is part elephant, part deer, part buffalo, part camel, and part sheep." Humbug!

Phineas Taylor Barnum knew that people enjoy seeing unusual people and animals and strange things from all over the world. And so he put unusual people in his sideshows. But sometimes he fooled the people with tricks—humbugs like the ones above.

He once humbugged people into paying to see an ordinary black cat by saying that it was cherry colored. The cat was the color of *black* cherries.

Sometimes, when the sideshows became too crowded, Barnum put up a sign: "This way to the Egress!" People didn't know that the word *egress* means "the way out," or "exit." They thought an egress was a new animal. When they went to see it, they found themselves outside.

Mr. Barnum was so proud of himself that he wrote a book telling how he did his humbugging. Yet in his shows he really did have some of the most unusual people, animals, and things from all over the world.

People didn't seem to mind being humbugged at Mr. Barnum's museum, since they could also see General Tom Thumb, a doll-sized little man who had stopped growing at an early age. The famous Siamese twins, Chang and Eng, were there, too, as well as a bearded lady, Mrs. Josephine Clofullia. Her beard was real—she was not a humbug.

And Americans were grateful to Mr. Barnum for bringing Jenny Lind, the "Swedish Nightingale," to this country. Her concert tour was such a success that many other great European singers followed.

But Barnum's biggest show of all was his traveling circus. Clowns, fierce animals, tiny people, and giants—the Barnum circus had them all.

If you liked this story, you'll like Circus *in Volume 3.*

BASEBALL

How Pitchers Fool Batters

"Strike two!" the umpire shouts.
The batter waits, wiggling his bat, ready to swing. The pitcher lifts his arms, stretches, and throws the ball. The batter swings and misses! It's a strikeout!

Even good batters sometimes strike out in baseball. The reason is that the pitcher never lets the batter know what kind of pitch he is going to throw. Sometimes he throws as hard as he can, sometimes not so hard, sometimes not hard at all. And sometimes he tricks the batter by making the ball curve a little bit as it nears home plate.

Most of the time—whether he throws a fast ball or a slow ball—the pitcher holds the ball the same way, with his first two fingers and thumb. But when he throws a curve or a slider (pitches that curve the ball toward or away from the batter), he holds the ball a little differently. He throws the curve with a twist of the wrist, letting the ball slide out from between his thumb and his first finger. That makes the ball spin, and the spin makes it curve.

A pitcher may hold the ball in still a different way—for a very special pitch. He takes the ball in his fingertips, using all his fingers, and just barely holds it with his fingernails. The pitcher looks as if he is throwing it hard; yet the ball comes very slowly and does not spin at all. You might think a pitch that does not spin at all would come straight across the plate, but it doesn't. Instead, air currents catch the seams of the ball—the places where it is sewn together—and make it turn right or left and bob up or down. Even the pitcher doesn't know exactly which way it is going to turn, and the batter can only guess.

BATS

It Flies, but It's Not a Bird

If bats could think about what kind of animal they are, they probably would be surprised to find out that they are not birds.

Bats are the only furry animals that can fly—without using an airplane, that is.

A bat's wings are really just long, thin fingers with a piece of skin—called a *membrane*—stretched between them.

A bat's wings have no feathers. A bat's body looks something like a mouse's body and is covered with soft fur.

A bat doesn't even have a bird's bill. It has a mouth with tiny, sharp teeth in it. It has a nose and furry ears. Some people call a bat a flying mouse—although it really isn't.

Bats fly very well with their unusual wings. You probably have seen them flying around in the early evening, zigging and zagging as they catch mosquitoes in the air. The insect-eating bats are very helpful to people. They eat billions and billions of harmful insects.

Other bats eat fruit or pollen from flowers. Some even catch small fish and eat them.

There are bats of many different colors. Most are brown, but some are blackish, orange, gray, grayish green, greenish white, red, or yellowish. Some are spotted or have two colors.

The large vampire bats, which live in hot jungles, can suck blood from other animals. They often carry germs that can make people sick, so people keep away from them. But most bats don't hurt anything except mosquitoes and other insects.

Bats can't see very well in the bright sunlight, so they sleep all day, hanging upside down in dark places, such as caves, hollow trees, and barns. They fly at night.

They can fly in places where it is so dark that they can't see. And yet, even in the pitch dark, they almost never bump into anything.

Why don't they?

Because they send out sounds as they fly. They aren't sounds that people can hear. But bats can hear them. The sounds go ahead of the flying bats and bounce back from anything that might be in their way. By hearing the echoes, bats can tell where things are in the dark.

In the north some bats *hibernate*—sleep a special long sleep—all winter long. Other northern bats, such as the red bat, simply fly to warmer places during the winter.

A baby bat drinks milk from its mother's breasts, as puppies or kittens do. When it is very young, the mother carries it with her. It clings to her fur as she flies through the air, searching for food.

*Do you want to learn how these fascinating creatures fly in the dark—
and how boats and planes can travel safely in the dark?
Read* Echoes *in Volume 5.*

BEACH

Sand Castles

Down, down on the beach, at the edge of the land
Where the ocean begins, where there's water and sand,

When the air's full of salt and the sky's full of sun,
You will know that the sand castle season's begun.

The first thing to do is to pick the right place—
Not too many people and plenty of space,

Where a wave is *whish-whishing* its foam on your toes
And packs the sand shiny wherever it goes.

You start out together by scooping up sand
And patting it down with the flat of your hand.

You build up your castle, while squatting for hours,
Making walls and a tunnel and bridges and towers.

And then you go searching along the wide shore
For shells that the waves have swept off the sea's floor.

Then back to your castle so high on the sand
To press in the shells that you hold in your hand,

Like candy and candles poked into a cake.
(But a castle is much more exciting to make.)

You don't need to hurry—you have the whole day
To make towers and turrets in every which way.

Dig a moat 'round your castle where water can curl.
Look out! There's a wave that is rolling to hurl

A white swirl of water against the high wall.
Look out—oh, look out, or your castle will fall!

The charge of the wave, with a *whoosh* and a *roar,*
Covers the castle and captures the shore.

The moat overflows, and the bridges are down.
If you've any toy people, watch out or they'll drown!

A tower is crumbling, and there goes a wall.
The flag on the flagpole's the last thing to fall.

And you wonder while watching it all wash away,
Should you bother to build when you know it can't stay?

But the answer rings clear, as you start a new one,
It's not just the having—it's building that's fun.

More About the Beach

Does the shore belong to the land or to the sea?

If it's hard for you to decide, maybe that's because the shore itself doesn't seem to know.

"Ocean waves, will you lie still?"
The ocean roars, "They won't!"
Waves play along the sandy shore.
You see them—then you don't.

The shore is the edge between the ocean and the land. It is the part that is sometimes under water and sometimes not. When the water moves in as far as it is going to go, we say that the tide is in, or that it is *high tide*. When the water draws back and the beach is as wide as it gets, we say the tide is out or that it is *low tide*. The water moves back and forth between high and low tide.

It might seem as if nothing could live along the shore. Think what would happen to any creature that did. Lying in the sand on the beach at low tide, it might get dried out by the hot sun.

Just a little later the rising tide might reach the creature and send waves crashing down on it again and again. Still later, when it was high tide, the creature would be living completely under the water.

Most of the plants and animals we know about can't live that way. They have to live *in* the water or *out* of the water—in the sea or on the land.

And yet as hard as such a life would seem, the shore is crowded with both plants and animals that live part of the time under the water and part of the time out of it.

Water animals that need to stay wet have to find ways to do this when the tide is low and they are left on the beach—out of the water.

When the tide moves out, many of the beach animals burrow deep into the sand to stay wet. Then they rest and wait for the return of the ocean with its rich supply of food. When it does return, they move back up out of the sand.

Some crabs and other sea creatures live in puddles that are trapped between rocks when the tide moves out.

Barnacles and mussels, which are stuck to rocks, open their shells when the tide moves in. They put out tiny *tentacles*, or feelers, to catch the still tinier water animals that they feed on.

As the tide moves out again, these and other shelled animals close their shells tightly to keep enough water inside to stay alive.

It isn't easy to live along the busy beach, belonging sometimes to the sea and sometimes to the land. But many animals—and plants, too—can do it.

BEARS

Watch Out for Bears!

    Did you ever see a bear dancing? Or wearing a funny hat and climbing a pole? Bears can be trained to do all kinds of tricks. In a circus you can see them wrestling, boxing, dancing, or even riding unicycles.
    But most bears are not the jolly, friendly creatures you see in a circus. Most bears are wild and dangerous animals that make their homes in forests and mountain country or on the ice and snow in the region around the North Pole.

It's true that in places like Yellowstone National Park some wild bears in the woods seem friendly. People in automobiles stop and watch bears begging for food along the road.

But it is dangerous to feed bears. They are so big and strong that while they are pawing you to find more food, they might claw you badly without meaning to. Candy and cake and hot dogs are not proper food for bears anyway. Too much of such food might even make them sick.

If you want to see wild bears close up, a good place to go is a zoo.

The biggest and strongest bear in the world—although not the fiercest—is the brown bear. Like other bears, it will eat almost anything—small animals, fish, nuts, berries, honey, and even ants.

The smallest and tamest bears live in warm deserts and jungles, where they climb trees to find honey, insects, and birds' eggs.

Of all the bears that roam the forests, the most dangerous is the big grizzly bear. Many bears will get out of your way if they see you coming—but not the grizzly. And it's fast! It can run faster than people.

No animal in the cold north is more feared than the giant, white-furred polar bear. Polar bears swim in the icy waters, catching fish, walrus, and seals. And they prowl over the icy land, catching anything they can. Polar bears will attack and kill people who get in their way. But people kill polar bears, too. Eskimos hunt them for food and for their warm furs.

Many bears take a long winter nap. They crawl into caves or hollow tree trunks or scoop out a place in the ground and cover it with leaves and grass.

There aren't very many of the big, big bears left in the world because hunters have been shooting them. Hunting laws have been passed to try to save the few that are left.

Do you like to read about animals and animal life?
Look under Animals *in Volume 1 or under* Zoo *in Volume 16.*

BEAVERS

The Busy Animal

This furry creature zigs and zags, twists and turns, as it skims through the water, using its back feet as flippers.

Picking up just the right size sticks and rocks for building its house, this animal has front feet that work as hands do.

It has a long, flat tail shaped like a canoe paddle—just right for steering in water and for leaning on when this fellow is gnawing down a tree.

Have you guessed what this animal is? It's a beaver—small, strong, and probably the cleverest builder in the animal world.

Without a saw, an ax, or a knife, a beaver can cut down a tree so big you couldn't wrap your arms around the trunk! It uses trees to build a dam across a river, making a private pond for beaver families.

How do beavers do all this hard work? Well, if you could look inside a beaver's mouth—don't try it, you'd get bitten!—you would see very long, very sharp front teeth. So long and so sharp that they can gnaw around a tree trunk in no time at all.

Crunch! Crack! Smash! Crash! Another tree ready for the beaver to gnaw into sticks and logs. (A beaver's front teeth aren't just sharp and strong—they never wear out. They keep right on growing as long as a beaver lives!)

Sometimes beavers manage to gnaw down a tree so that it falls in the water. But if it misses, the beavers don't seem to be bothered. They dig a canal—a water path—cut the tree into logs with their teeth, and float the logs to the right place for building a dam.

Beavers work much as construction workers do. Each has a job. When all the logs are pushed together, the beavers plaster the cracks with mud and rocks.

Time for a rest? Not for beavers. It's time for house building! Scurrying back and forth to gather sticks and stones . . . clawing for mud to pack their houses tight and safe . . . beavers make wonderful houses.

A snug dry room above the water is lined with moss and soft shredded bark—perfect for raising beaver babies.

The storage place for winter food is underwater. Beavers don't waste any part of a tree—they even use the bark for food!

If you should see one beaver, you can be sure that other beavers are close by. They build together. They live together. And they stay safe together!

If a beaver spots an enemy (wildcats and wolves hunt beavers for food, but men hunt them for their silky fur), it slaps its tail as hard as it can on the water. *Smack!* Beavers know that sound means trouble. They race for the water, dive in, and swim out to their houses.

Are you ever "busy as a beaver"?

"Busy as a beaver" is an old, old saying that means working hard. And no one seems to work harder than beavers!

You can read about man-made Dams *in Volume 4.*

BEES

A Hive Is a House for Bees

Hum-m-m-m-m-m-m and buz-z-z-z-z-z-z.
Buz-z-z-z-z-z-z and hum-m-m-m-m-m-m.
Here and there and everywhere
The honeybees are flying.
Where are they going?
Why?

They are following a queen bee to a new home. Not all of the bees will go with the queen to find the new home. Some will stay in the old hive with another queen.

Let's follow the bees that are flying away.

"They're going this way! Hurry, hurry, or we'll lose them."

"Now they're in this tree. We'll need the ladder."

"When I give the word, shake the branch hard."

"Now! Shake hard!"

When most of the bees and their queen are in the hive, the beekeeper will cover the hive and carry it home. Or, if he has to go very far, he will take it home in a truck. Now he will have two hives of bees instead of one.

A hive is a house for bees. It's where they live and make honey.

If the beekeeper had not gone after his bees and taken them home in the new hive, the bees would have flown away and found a hive of their own. They might have set up housekeeping in a hollow tree, or in a cave, or even between the walls of somebody's house if they could find a hole to crawl through.

All bees used to be wild bees, and none lived in man-made hives. The big fat *buzzing* bumblebees still make their homes under the ground, or in old stumps, or in dried grass. They may even move into an empty mouse nest or a chipmunk burrow.

Bears and a few other wild animals still rob the wild bees to get honey. A bear's skin and fur is so thick that bee stings don't hurt very much.

Once in a while men chop down a tree to get the honey in it. Sometimes they build a fire near the tree to smoke the bees out before they take the honey. But most of the honey that people eat today comes from beehives that men have made.

Today there are bee farms with row after row of beehives that look like little houses on crowded streets. The beekeeper takes care of the bees, and sometimes moves the hives around on trucks to places where there are flowers or blossoms. In this way he helps the bees to make their honey. He never takes all the honey from the hive. He leaves some for the bees to eat.

If you could look inside one of these busy beehives, what do you think you'd see?

You'd see bees, of course. And you'd see little six-sided rooms, or *cells*. The bees build these cells with wax—*beeswax*. We don't know exactly how they do it, but bees make the wax inside their bodies.

Inside the little rooms the bees store honey and special bee food, and keep the tiny eggs from which the baby bees will hatch.

There are rooms for the worker bees, and a very special BIG room for the queen bee.

Most of the bees' work is done in the spring and summer. Then the honey is made and stored and the queen bee lays most of her eggs.

Besides the *queen,* the biggest bee of all, there are two other kinds of bees—*drones* and *workers*. The drones are bigger than the workers, and they have no stingers. They don't do any of the work, either. But one of them mates with the queen and is the father of all the workers in the hive.

Each of the workers has a special job. Some bees build the rooms in the hive. Some keep the hive clean. Some take care of the baby bees. Some take care of the queen.

Some bees are soldiers. They guard the hive, and chase away other bees, or wasps, or any other insects that might try to get in and steal the honey.

Other bees fly out to visit flowers and blossoms. They bring back pollen and nectar to be made into bee food or honey.

Some bees even stay by the door and flap their wings fast to blow cool air through the hive.

Bees don't like it *too* cool. So in the wintertime they pile one on top of another in one part of the hive, and move their bodies and six legs against each other to keep warm.

Can you guess who stays in the middle of the pile to keep warmest? The queen!

Do you like to read about the way insects live?
You'll like reading Ants *in Volume 1.*

BEES

Honeybee at Work

B-z-z-z-z-z-z-z-z-z-z-z-z-z-z. . . .
Honeybee at work!
The bee flies from blossom to blossom, gathering food for other bees. And without knowing it, the bee is helping make a delicious food for us to eat.

You know one of the foods that bees make. *Honey*.

When we think of bees, we think of honey. But it isn't honey that the bees are making here.

They haven't started making it yet. They are only gathering a sweet juice called *nectar* to take back to the hive, where other bees will make it into honey.

In gathering the nectar, these bees are actually helping make apples.

It doesn't sound reasonable, does it?

Well, here is the way it works. It starts with something called *pollen*.

Pollen looks like dust. It grows in a flower.

If pollen from one flower falls on a special part of another flower, something wonderful starts to happen. A fruit will begin to grow!

Such fruits as apples, oranges, pears, and peaches grow when the right pollen for each fruit reaches just the right flower. And that's where the honeybee comes in.

When a bee crawls around inside a flower, pollen sticks to the bee's fuzzy legs. Later, when the bee is crawling around inside another flower, some specks of the pollen may rub off onto just the right part of the flower. And then the fruit will start growing.

The bee doesn't know it's being so helpful. But without bees to move the pollen, there wouldn't be so much good fruit to eat.

Soon after some of the pollen falls on the special place in the flower, the petals drop off and the rest of the flower begins to change.

In a few weeks a tiny fruit is formed.

And a few weeks later the fruit is big and ripe and ready to eat.

If you liked this story,
read about **Flowers** *in Volume 6.*

BEETHOVEN, LUDWIG VAN

The Lonely Giant

School was out! On this fine spring day, a group of schoolboys in Vienna were running along the street.

"Look!" one of the boys cried. "There's the crazy man!"

A short, stocky man in an old green coat was walking ahead of them. His long hair looked as if it had never been combed. His pockets were stuffed with papers and pencils and all sorts of things. Sometimes he pulled out a paper and scribbled on it, talking to himself. Sometimes he growled like a bear, and sometimes he laughed and waved his arms around.

The boys watched the strange man as he went down the street. Then the boys ran on. But one boy, Franz, dropped behind. He wanted to stay with his friends, but he had to go home and practice the piano. His parents had promised that if he practiced every day they would take him to the concert to hear the music of the great composer Ludwig van Beethoven, who had not appeared in public for many years. And Franz didn't want to miss seeing the great man—a giant in the world of music.

The night of the concert came. Most of the important people in Vienna—princes, barons, and dukes—were there.

Franz stood on tiptoe to see the stage. He noticed that even "the crazy man" was there. In his old green coat he walked right up onto the stage, and nobody stopped him!

Franz saw him stand before the orchestra and pick up the baton. He couldn't believe his eyes. Was "the crazy man" the great Beethoven? The orchestra began to play the Ninth Symphony.

The people had never heard such music. Indeed, this was the first performance of the Ninth Symphony and some of its music is considered among the greatest Beethoven ever wrote. The audience was impressed by the composer's new ideas.

When the orchestra stopped playing, the people shouted, "Bravo!" and clapped. But Beethoven couldn't hear them. The poor composer was deaf. He could hear neither the beautiful music he had written nor the cheering of the crowd. One of the performers gently turned him around so that he could *see* the people clapping.

Beethoven had a sad and lonely life. When he became deaf, he hid. He talked to people and made friends only through his music. Today, though he has been dead for more than a hundred years, his music still makes friends for him.

Other stories about famous composers may be found under Bach *in this volume,* Mozart *in Volume 10, and* Stravinsky *in Volume 14.*

87

BELL, ALEXANDER GRAHAM

The First Telephone

"Go down the hall, Mr. Watson. Let's try it again."

Mr. Watson went down the hall and waited in a tiny room. How many, many times he had waited until the little wooden box in front of him hummed or buzzed.

"Hums and buzzes," he sighed. "That's all I ever hear—hums and buzzes."

Suddenly the box buzzed again. But this time, with the buzzing sound, came words.

"Mr. Watson, come here. I want you," the box squawked anxiously.

Mr. Watson didn't know whether to laugh or to cry. The voice coming through the box sounded worried, as if Mr. Bell might be in trouble. Mr. Watson ran down the hall to the laboratory, shouting, "It works! It works!"

Mr. Bell forgot all about the acid he had spilled on his trousers. "Good!" he exclaimed. "Good!" It was March 10, 1876—the day that Alexander Graham Bell's invention, the telephone, finally worked.

Although most people remember Alexander Graham Bell for his invention of the telephone, he experimented with many things. He tried new ways of teaching deaf children how to speak, found different uses for electricity, and studied ways of traveling by air.

If you're interested in reading how some famous discoveries have come about, look under Inventions *in Volume 8.*

BELL, ALEXANDER GRAHAM

More About Alexander Graham Bell

Alexander Graham Bell was interested in the troubles of deaf people—people who can't hear. Both his father and his grandfather had spent their lives studying human speech and teaching the deaf to speak.

Just a few years before he invented the telephone, Alexander opened a school for teachers of the deaf.

Alexander Graham Bell was also interested in electricity. He experimented with things he hoped might help the deaf to hear. These experiments gave him the idea for the telephone.

In his invention, a sound—such as a person speaking—made a thin circle of metal *vibrate*, or move back and forth very fast. The vibrating part changed the way electricity moved through the wires from one phone to another. A loud sound sent more electricity through the wires than a soft sound.

These electric changes made a part in the listener's phone vibrate, which created a sound very much like the sound the speaker made into *his* phone. That's pretty much how the telephone still works today.

To the person listening, it seems as though the sound is coming through the wire. But it isn't—only electricity is! The electricity is changed back into sound *inside* the listener's telephone.

When someone invents something, that is only the beginning. Men all over the world immediately look for ways to make the invention work better. That is exactly what happened with the telephone.

If Mr. Bell were alive today, he would probably be surprised and pleased to see how his telephone has been improved.

Now telephone calls can be made to millions of people all over the world. On some calls the message goes through wires inside huge cables stretched across the ocean bottom. On other calls the message is sent by radio and bounced off communications satellites high above the Earth.

Picture phones allow the people talking to see one another if they wish.

And there's no telling what new things the telephone will do in the future, thanks to inventors.

*If you liked this story,
read* Inventions *in Volume 8.*

BELLS

Ding-Dong Bell

*With rings on her fingers
and bells on her toes
She shall have music
wherever she goes.*

Ting-a-ling go the tiny bells. Little girls wear them on bracelets on their wrists. Cats wear them on collars around their necks. (The birds hear the bells and know the cat is coming. The birds fly safely away.)
And what about all the other bells?
Ding-dong-bing-bong go the big bells in the church steeples and high bell towers.
Clang-clang-clang-clang go the bells on the fire engine.
Ca-ling-ca-ling go the bells on the bicycles.
Ri-ng-ng-ng-ng-ng-ng go the telephone and the doorbell.
Jingle-jangle-cabangle-ding-ding-ding goes the alarm clock, loud enough to wake you up.

The first bells were made of thin pieces of metal held together with tiny metal pins. When these bells sounded, they just went *plunk-plunk* and could be heard only by those who were close by.

Finally, someone found out that a bell made in one piece and with a special shape would give a loud, clear, pleasing sound and would echo its ring for a long time.

At first, most of the bells were hung around the necks of cows and sheep to help the farmer find them when they were lost or straying. Bells are still used in this way, but as men made better and better bells, they found many new uses for them, too.

Bells were put in clocks to strike the time. They were rung to call people to important town meetings. Bells were put in high steeples to call people to church, and children to school. When people were happy about something, they rang the bells fast. When they were sad—if somebody died or if a battle in a war was lost—they rang the bells slowly.

Finally, steeples were built that held a great many bells, each of a different size, and each ringing a different sound. The men who rang these bells pulled ropes from below. They would play tunes with the bells. Sometimes one man would ring three bells—one with each hand and one with his foot. (Not the foot he was standing on!)

In many parts of the world, bells are still used for some of these things.

Today in some large churches and bell towers, the bells are rung by an organ player. He touches the keys of the organ, and the bells in the steeple play the tune.

In many places in the world, bell buoys mark the way for ships. The waves lift the floating buoy up and down and from side to side, making the bell ring. Even in a fog or at night, sailors can hear the bell and know where to steer their ship to keep from running into the rocks.

Some bells are run by electricity. On the inside of an electric doorbell, there is a round metal ball called the *clapper*. When someone pushes the button outside the house, electricity goes through the wire and makes the clapper knock against the bell, again and again—very quickly— which makes the bell ring.

95

BIRDS

What Is a Bird?

Ron was a boy who read a lot of books, and he liked to make up riddles. They seemed like silly riddles at first. But the answers were never as easy as you thought they were going to be.

Here is one of his riddles—"How can you tell if a bird is a bird?"

"That's the *nothingest* riddle I ever heard," Janie told him. "Anybody can tell if a bird is a bird."

"Okay, tell me," Ron said.

"Because it flies—that's why."

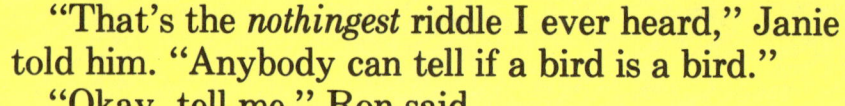

"But not all birds fly," Ron said. "Ostriches don't. Penguins don't."

"But they do have wings," Janie said. "So that's how you can tell if a bird is a bird—if it has wings."

"What about a bat?"

"Hey, that's right. A bat has wings and can fly, but it's not a bird."

Ron nodded. "Lots of things have wings—moths, butterflies, bees . . . even airplanes."

Janie was thinking hard. "Hey, this isn't as easy as it seems, is it?"

"Try again," Ron said. "How can you tell if a bird is a bird?"

"Because it sings?"

"No," Ron answered. "Crickets and teakettles and lots of things sing. Even a grasshopper makes a kind of song by rubbing its wings and legs together."

Janie laughed. "Sure. Even *I* sing, and I'm not a bird."

"And some birds don't sing at all. They just peep a little or squawk."

"*I* know," Janie said. "Because it has a beak. Most animals have teeth. But a bird has a beak instead."

"That's a pretty good guess," Ron said. "But some insects have mouths that are called *beaks*. Guess again."

"All right, then—because of its legs."

"What's so special about its legs?"

"The number, silly. A dog and a horse and a giraffe and a rabbit and almost every animal you can think of has four legs.

Insects have six. I know because one time you told me. Centipedes have so many legs that they're hard to count. A bird has only two."

"But so do you, and you're not a bird."

"Hey, this is getting harder all the time—"

"No, it's really easy. Think before you guess next time."

"Well-ll—a bird lays eggs—"

"Yes, but so do frogs, turtles, ants, alligators, and some snakes."

"They make nests—"

"Not all of them. Some birds lay their eggs in other birds' nests. Some lay them on the ground."

"Okay," Janie said, "I give up. I guess there isn't any way to tell if a bird is a bird."

"Sure there is," Ron said. "Don't give up, Janie. It's easy. Think. What is it that birds have that no other animal has?"

"Feathers?"

"You guessed it! Feathers! Birds are the only animals that have feathers. If you see something with feathers on it—big or little, flying or swimming or walking—you can be sure it's a bird."

To learn about some unusual birds, look up
Ostriches *in Volume 11 and* Penguins *in Volume 12.*

BIRDS

Welcome, Birds

Would you like to speak bird language? Would you like to be able to say, "Welcome, birds"?

You don't need to learn how to whistle. You don't need to learn any strange-sounding words.

The way to say "Welcome, birds" is to attach a *bird feeder* to a tree in your yard or to your windowsill. You can buy a bird feeder at the hardware store, or ask someone to help you make one.

A good place to put a bird feeder is on a tree limb that's low enough for you to reach. Or you might choose a windowsill that is close to some bushes. Birds don't feel safe in the open. They like lots of hiding places nearby.

Now ask your mother if you can have a handful of oatmeal or bread crumbs, or a big dab of peanut butter. Most birds like these foods as much as you like an ice cream cone. Birds also like unsalted nuts, sunflower seeds, and *suet*. Suet is a kind of dry, hard fat that you can buy from the butcher.

After you've filled your bird feeder, don't ring the dinner bell. Don't call out, "Soup's on!" Just wait. And be patient. It may take the birds a few days or even a week to discover their new "restaurant." But once they do, business will be brisk.

And you'll be talking the language that birds understand.

Don't put salty foods in your feeder. Salt makes birds uncomfortably thirsty and may even kill them.

Don't put suet in your feeder after winter is over. Fat is too rich for birds in warm weather and makes them sick.

Do put food in your feeder whenever it is empty. There may be some birds that depend upon finding the food you have left for them.

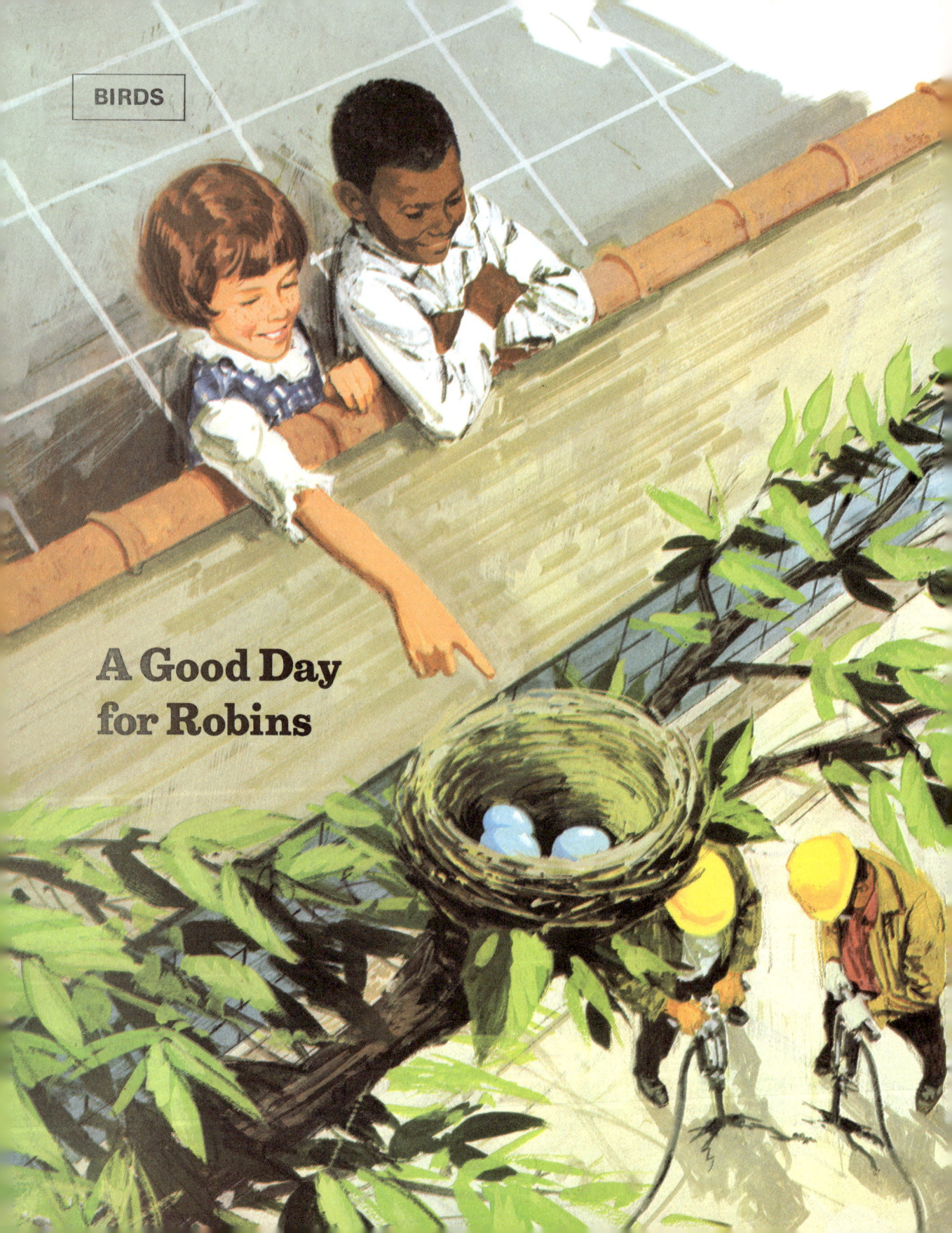

It's an egg, that's what it is. And it's all smashed!"

"I'll bet it's a *robin's* egg," Lisa whispered.

"How can you tell?" Jeff asked.

"It's kind of blue green like robins' eggs are. Let's find the nest."

It was recess time at Jeff and Lisa's school. Most of the other children were standing on the curb with their teacher, watching workmen get ready to drill holes in the street. One of the workers tried his drill. The loud noise of the drill went *rat-a-tat, rat-a-tat* over and over.

Jeff and Lisa looked up into the branches of the tree. It was a windy day late in spring, and the branches seemed to dance in the sunlight.

"Oh, I hope the wind doesn't knock the nest out of the tree," Lisa said in a worried voice.

The two children ran up the schoolhouse stairs so they could look down into the branches.

"There it is!" Lisa yelled as she pointed.

"*Shh!* You'll scare the mother bird," Jeff warned. "See, she's flying away."

"Just to find food, I'll bet. Look! Still some eggs in the nest."

They both counted. There were three very blue eggs resting in a soft bed of grass and twigs and feathers all stuck together with mud.

"Let's tell Miss Barton and the other kids," Jeff said. "Wouldn't it be great to see the baby birds when they first hatch from the eggs?"

Their teacher, Miss Barton, looked up when Jeff and Lisa came skipping toward her.

"Hey, Miss Barton! Guess what! We found a robin's nest. One egg was smashed, but there are three more in the nest." Lisa was almost dancing in her excitement. "Imagine! A robin's nest in the middle of the city. Miss Barton, please tell the workmen not to drill. It will scare the mother!"

Mr. Ambrose, the foreman of the street crew, looked up and said, "Well, Miss Barton, I don't know if the drills bother birds. But I've got to get on with this job. It could take weeks for those eggs to hatch."

"Only *two* weeks," Jeff said. "We just studied birds in class."

Mr. Stewart, who had stopped cutting the grass to listen, said, "If that's true, they should hatch any day now. I saw those eggs about two weeks ago, it seems to me."

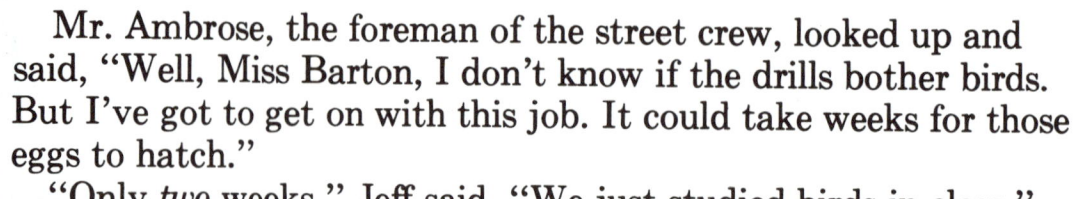

"We love Mr. Stewart!" the children cheered. "We love Mr. Stewart!"

The street crew foreman took off his hard hat and wiped his forehead. He looked at the other workers, and they looked at him. Lisa held her breath. No one said anything. Then the foreman shrugged and began to laugh. And then everyone smiled.

"Well, kids," he said, "it just so happens that we've got some work to do on some pipes in the next block. I suppose we could fix them first."

"Could you! Oh, thank you, Mr. Ambrose," Lisa cried.

"We love Mr. Ambrose! We love Mr. Ambrose!" the children chanted as they skipped around looking up at the nest.

"Better have those eggs hatched in two days," Mr. Ambrose called after them. "We'll have to come back and finish up here pretty soon."

The next day the children could hardly wait to see if the eggs had hatched. Lisa and Jeff tiptoed up the stairs first.

"Just eggs. No babies," Lisa said with disappointment as she peered down.

"We still have one more day," Jeff said, trying to make himself feel better.

They watched as the mother bird settled over her eggs to keep them warm. A few minutes later, the father bird swooped down with a worm for her to eat.

"Maybe tomorrow," Miss Barton said.

Lisa woke up very early the next morning. So did most of the other children. They all knew that Mr. Ambrose had to finish fixing the street the next day.

"I'm afraid to look," Lisa said, as she and Jeff climbed the stairs, going slower with every step.

"Me, too," said Jeff. "But we might as well know the worst."

Lisa closed her eyes tightly when she got to the top of the stairs. Then she opened them and looked down.

There were three skinny baby birds in the nest. Each had its tiny beak wide open.

"Hooray, hooray!" Lisa and Jeff shouted.

Some of the other children had joined them now. Everyone clapped and jumped up and down. Even Miss Barton joined the cheering. Just then, the mother and father birds flew down with worms for the babies to eat. As soon as they dropped the worms into the babies' beaks, they flew off again to find more food.

"I think we should tell Mr. Ambrose," Miss Barton said.

And so a crowd of very happy boys and girls hurried down the street to the next block. As soon as he saw their beaming faces, Mr. Ambrose knew that everything was all right.

Rat-a-tat, rat-a-tat. The drills shook up and down as they tore into the street.

"We love Mr. Ambrose!" the children cried.

The workmen winked and smiled at each other. "I think it's going to be a good day," Mr. Ambrose said.

"It already is!" Lisa answered.

Robins aren't the only birds that build nests in the city.

Wherever it's high and flat and sheltered, that's where pigeons build their nests. They'll use anything they can find to build them—crumbled rock, weeds, mud, or grass. Some pigeons don't bother making nests at all. They lay their eggs out in the open. If you look under a concrete city bridge, you might see a pigeon nest.

Cardinal nests are hard to find. They're usually hidden in the thick branches of small evergreen trees. (It's not hard to find father cardinals. They're bright red!)

Sparrows build grassy nests almost any place that is small and snug—over the outside part of air conditioners, under eaves, and in the rain gutters of houses.

A bird's apartment house on a high pole is just right for purple martins. People often build these birdhouses and hope a family of purple martins will move in! (They eat pesky mosquitoes.)

Want to know more? Read about Eggs *in Volume 5.*

BIRDS

The Boy Who Hated Cages

John James Audubon closed the door behind him quietly. He looked around the room. The spring sun, brighter than a thousand golden candles, lit every corner. John James could see that no one else was here. The only sound was that of the three goldfinches, scratching the bottom of their cage.

It was a very large bird cage—almost as large as the table on which it sat. Its bars were as slender as flower stems. Some people might have thought the cage was beautiful, but to John James it was a prison.

He tiptoed across the room toward it. Stiffening a thin shoulder against the table, he began to shove. *Kerr-eech!* He straightened up. Had anyone heard the scraping of the table legs?

The goldfinches fluttered wildly in their cage.

"Don't be afraid, little birds," he whispered. "I'm your friend."

He gave the table another shove and then another, until it was next to the window. He opened the window, then opened the door of the cage. The goldfinches hopped out.

"Fly!" John James said, holding back the window curtains for them. "Go! You are free!"

John James watched the birds flutter from the windowsill. They were stiff and clumsy, unused to spreading their wings. But each managed to fly to a low branch on the nearest tree. They looked around at the wide blue sky. They rubbed their stubby beaks against soft curling leaves. *"Per-chic-o-ree!"* Their song made the day even more beautiful.

The boy, listening, was able to forget how hard it would be to explain to his father what he had done.

Later, John James' father discovered that the birds were gone. "Why didn't you ask me if you might set the birds free?" he asked.

"I was afraid you'd say no——"

"Am I so unreasonable?"

"N-n-no," said John James. "But I just couldn't tell you how unhappy it made me to see those birds in a cage."

"I loved those goldfinches, too," said his father. "Each one had different shades of color. And yet they blended together—like a beautiful painting."

"I know! I know!" said John James. "They were like this."

He handed his father a drawing of the goldfinches. His father held the big piece of sketch paper, studying it carefully.

"Do you like it?" John James finally asked.

His father looked up from the drawing. "I have never seen our goldfinches look more alive! Your drawing has captured and held them more than any cage. How did you manage to make them so real, so exact?"

"I watched them as they hopped about in the cage," John James said. "I watched other goldfinches, too—ones that were out in the open. I watched how they moved their wings, how they placed their toes on the branches, how they held their heads when they sang. Then I imagined our goldfinches as they would be if they'd been free—and I drew them."

His father smiled. "If you had shown me this picture first, I would have set them free myself. I hope you will draw more pictures of birds."

John James smiled back at his father. "I want to draw every kind of bird in the world. Each one is so beautiful—but cages, *all* kinds of cages, are so ugly!"

These scenes from the life of John James Audubon happened in France when he was a very young boy—many years ago. Later, when he was 18 years old, he came to live in the United States. It was a young country then. Great pathless forests covered large parts of it. In these forests lived many birds. It was a dream come true for Audubon to live in such a place.

John James Audubon did not succeed in painting every kind of bird in the world, but he did paint hundreds and hundreds of them. He lived to see his paintings published in four huge volumes called the elephant edition, because the books are so big.

Audubon always painted birds life-size. He painted each bird so carefully and skillfully that you can almost feel their tiny hearts pumping as they plunge into the waves of wind and cloud.

When you look at one of Audubon's paintings, you imagine you hear the bird singing. You imagine what it would be like to run your finger among its sun-flecked feathers. Grown-ups and children everywhere have come to know and love birds because of Audubon's beautiful pictures. People have formed clubs called Audubon Societies to study and protect birds.

Children have their own Audubon Junior Clubs. They explore the world of birds—the trees and bushes, the shores and meadows—and often they draw birds. When you are a little older, perhaps you will want to join one of these clubs.

From John J. Audubon, "Birds of America," with permission from the National Audubon Society

BLACKWELL, ELIZABETH

The First Woman Doctor

Is your doctor a man or a woman?

Most doctors in the United States and other countries are men. Still, there are many thousands of woman doctors working in the United States. But more than a hundred years ago, there were none.

The first woman to study at a medical school in the United States was Elizabeth Blackwell. She did much to make it possible for other women to become doctors, too. But it wasn't easy for her to get started in a job that, at the time, was held only by men.

Elizabeth decided to become a doctor around 1847, when she was about 26 years old. She worked as a school teacher for a

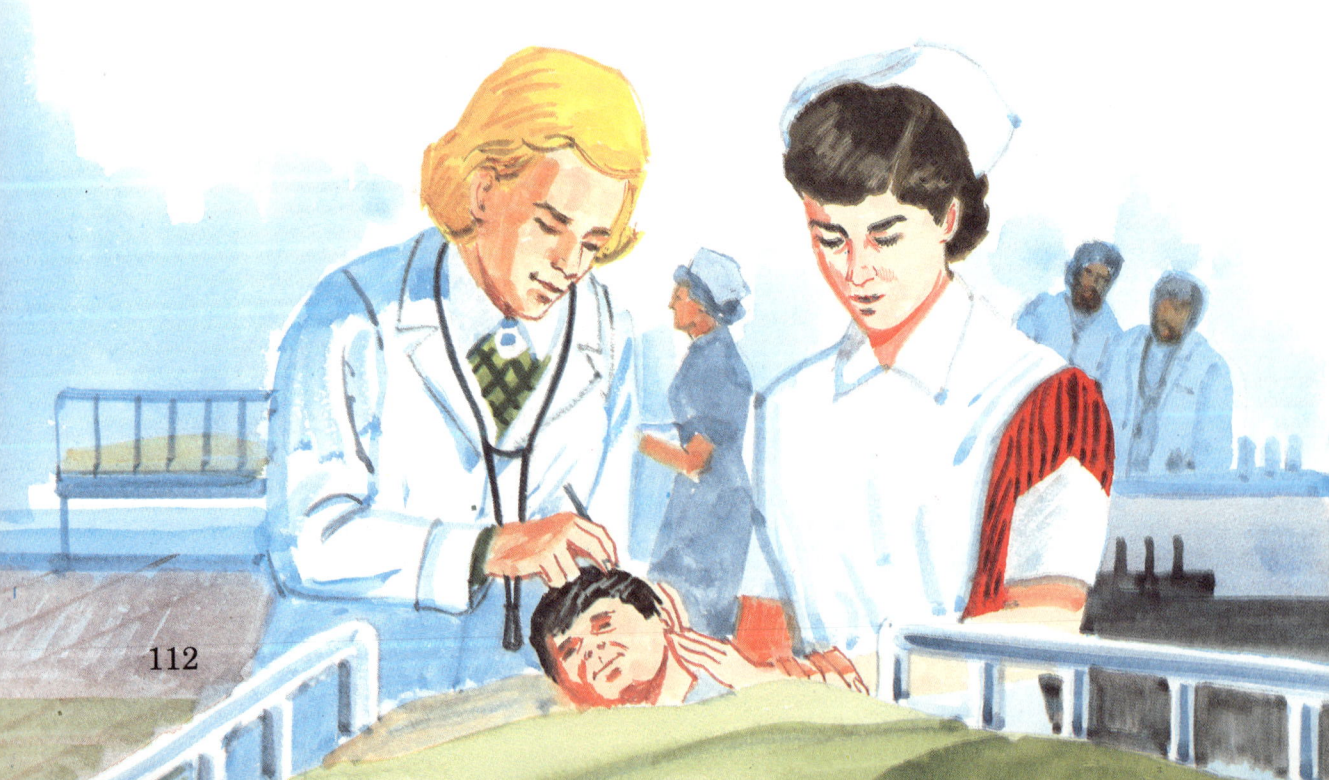

time to save enough money to pay for her own schooling. But when she tried to get into the well-known medical colleges in the United States, she was turned down.

The teachers who taught medicine during her day were all men. Many of these men didn't think it was right for a woman to be a doctor. Quite a few of them thought that a woman should stay at home and raise a family. A few were even afraid that a woman doctor would make too much money from other women.

Only a few of the teachers tried to help her get into medical school. But they knew that it would be very hard for her to do so. Two teachers said that she might get in if she were to dress up like a man and pretend to be one. But Elizabeth didn't think it was right to fool people. She wanted to be honest.

After she had written and spoken to teachers in most of the medical colleges in the United States, Elizabeth finally found a school in western New York state that was willing to take her. She became the only woman in a class of 150 men.

Many people laughed at the idea of a woman becoming a doctor. But the other students at the school soon found that Elizabeth took her work seriously, and they saw nothing wrong with the idea. When she finished her schooling 2 years later, Elizabeth became the first woman in America to earn the title, Doctor of Medicine.

Elizabeth and her sister Emily, who also became a doctor, opened a hospital for women in New York City. The sisters hired other women to work in the hospital. Knowing how difficult it was for a woman to become a doctor, some years later Elizabeth and Emily started a school for training women doctors at the hospital. More than anyone else, Dr. Elizabeth Blackwell opened the doors of medical science to women.

BOLÍVAR, SIMÓN

Hero of Many Nations

Once in a country named Venezuela there lived a man who had a big dream. He wanted *all* the countries of South America to be free so that they could join together to become one strong country.

The man with this big dream was Simón Bolívar.

From all over the world men who heard about Simón Bolívar's dream came to help him. Many of them had to sail across the ocean and then hunt for him in forests and on prairies where the grass grew higher than men's heads.

At one time these men marched on foot with Bolívar, wading for seven days through floodwaters up to their waists and then crossing high mountains where the icy wind blew against them. Tired and hungry, wanting to rest, they arrived finally in a country named New Granada (now Colombia). They surprised the big Spanish Army. Fighting fiercely, they beat the Spanish and freed New Granada.

Simón Bolívar fought many battles to free other countries in South America. He lost some battles, but he won many of them. Everywhere he rode on his great war-horse the people ran out into the streets to shout and cheer for this man who risked his life to help them. He was their hero and their leader.

Simón Bolívar's dream of freeing the countries from Spain came true, but even he was never able to make the people of the different countries join together as one nation. Nevertheless, he is the most important hero in South America. In his honor one of the countries there was named Bolivia. And in his own country, Venezuela, the paper money, instead of being called francs or pounds or dollars, is called *bolivars!*

*Other stories about South America may be found
under* Amazon *in Volume 1
and* Rio de Janeiro *in Volume 13.*

BOOKS

Who's in the Library?

A first adventure in reading

The books in your library were written by many different men and women from all over the world. Some lived long, long ago. Some are still alive today. Even those who are not alive can still tell you things—*in their books*.

If all of these writers could suddenly be in your library, they would fill all the rooms, hang out the windows, and cover the roof! They would fill the street and spread through the neighborhood!

Isn't it lucky that libraries are filled with books instead of writers? The writers couldn't be in all libraries at once.

But their books can.

In nearly every large town and city, people can go to libraries to read the wise and beautiful and exciting and funny things that have been written.

BOOKS

Tim Says

My brother Tim, who's now eleven,
   Began to read when he was seven.
I'm only six—but soon, says Tim,
   I shall be reading just like him.
If you know where, says Tim, to look,
   You're always bound to find a book
That tells you almost instantly
   —No matter what the thing may be—
Exactly what you want to know.
   Why does it rain? Why does it snow?
Find out, says Tim, in books on science.
   And Tim says other books have giants;
And some have elves and wicked witches,
   Magic lamps and buried riches.
In one a boy named Tom was brave
   Till he was rescued from a cave.
Tim says he's read a hundred tales
   Of animals, from mice to whales;
Of horses flying through the sky;
   Of little men six inches high;
Cannibals and Indian scouts;
   Great victories or bloody routs
In battles long ago; or fights
   On horseback between armored knights.
The books are waiting on the shelf.
   "Soon you'll be reading them yourself,"
Says Tim; and what Tim says is so.
   Look out, books! Here I come! Let's go!

If you liked this poem, look under Library
in Volume 9 and Reading *in Volume 13.*

BOOKS

More About Books

The way people make books has changed a lot since long ago, when a book didn't look anything like the one you're reading right now.

In ancient times most books looked something like a roll of paper towels. The roll might be made of animal skins, thin strips of bark from trees, or a thick kind of paper made from special plants.

Often the words and pictures were painted with a brush. Sometimes the words were written with a pen made from a large feather. It usually took weeks or months to make just one book. Today giant presses can print thousands of books in an hour.

But long before the presses start to print, a lot of other work has to be done. After a writer writes the words, an *editor* must decide the size of the book and the number of pages. The editor also makes sure that the writing is the way it is supposed to be and that all the words are spelled correctly.

Should the book have pictures? How many? Should they be black and white or in color? Some of the pictures may be drawings. Others may be photographs.

A book designer chooses the *type,* or the kind of letters that are printed in the book. There are many different kinds of type.

The kind of type chosen depends on the kind of book it is. The size of type can be LARGE or small or in between. Very large type uses a lot of space. Very small type is hard to read.

There are many different ways of getting the type, drawings, and photographs for a book ready for a printing press, but the last step is to make a *plate,* a sheet of thin metal or other material for each color of ink to be used in the book. Sometimes the plates are quite large. They will hold the ink for up to 8 or 16 or even more pages. When plates are made, the book is ready to be printed.

There are many different kinds of printing presses. One is a *web press.* The paper, which comes in a long roll called a *web,* passes through the press, going over, under, and between many rollers. The printing plates are wrapped tightly around the rollers.

There are usually two rollers for each color of ink used in the book. By using pairs of rollers, web presses can print both sides of pages as the paper passes through the press just one time.

After the pages have been printed on the paper, a machine cuts and folds the paper into sections, and then another machine puts the sections together to make a book. Other machines are used to sew or glue or staple the sections together. Then the pages are trimmed to make the edges smooth and neat.

Covers are made from many different types of materials by a number of different machines. When a machine finally puts the book and its cover together, the big job is done.

BOONE, DANIEL

How Daniel Boone Learned from Nature

When Daniel Boone was a little boy, his family lived in a cabin right on the edge of the woods. Dan got to wondering about the woods and began pestering people with questions.

"How big is the forest? What's on the other side of it?" he would ask.

Nobody could tell him because nobody knew.

"I guess I'll just have to find out for myself," Dan said. His mother worried about him. "That boy is never going to learn anything useful hanging around the woods all the time," she used to say.

But Dan found some good teachers in the woods.

He met some raccoons that taught him how to climb a tree. He met some otters that taught him how to swim and fish. An owl taught him how to hoot, and a badger how to hide in the grass.

From the beavers he learned how to build a snug house out of sticks and mud. From the deer he learned how to run fast. He learned what wild growing things were good to eat and where to find them. After he had learned all of these things—and some Indian tricks, too—he was just about the best woodsman around.

By the time Daniel Boone was a grown man, a lot of people were asking the same questions he used to ask: "How big is the forest? And what is beyond it?"

But now there was someone to answer them. Daniel Boone.
"On the other side of the woods and over the mountains is a place the Indians call *Kentake* [Kentucky]," Boone told them. "It's a country with fine land and rolling green hills and rivers."

When the people heard about this place, they wanted to go there. They asked Boone to lead the way, and he said he would.

He rounded up some men and hacked out a path through the big woods that was wide enough for people to travel over on horses, and later with wagons. He cut his path through a gap in the mountains—Cumberland Gap—and followed an old Indian trail and a path worn down by herds of buffalo.

Later this path over the mountains became known as the Wilderness Road or Boone's Way. Pioneer families poured over it to settle in Kentucky. Boone and his family settled there, too, in the town named after him, Boonesboro.

But Daniel Boone the pathfinder never stayed very long anywhere. Until the end of his life, he kept making paths and finding new places.

You may read about another famous pioneer under Davy Crockett *in Volume 3.*

BREAD

Fresh from the Bakery

One of the best smells in the whole world is the smell that comes floating out the door of a bakery early in the morning.

What is that smell? It's bread baking. You usually smell it only in the early morning because the baker makes his bread while you are sleeping at night. At dawn he takes the bread out of the oven, and his customers have truly fresh bread.

Making bread takes time. First the baker mixes a lot of flour with some milk or water, butter and sugar, a bit of salt, and some yeast. He may use a big machine for the mixing.

The machine stirs and stretches the gooey dough, making it tough and a little rubbery. This stirring is called *kneading*.

Then the baker puts the dough aside, and the yeast begins to work.

Yeast is the magic ingredient. A cake or package of yeast is really many, many tiny plants all ready to grow if given the chance. In the wet, warm bread dough, the yeast plants get the chance. As they grow, they give off a gas called *carbon dioxide*. The bubbles of this gas stretch the dough around them, and the bread dough begins to swell up and up, getting bigger and bigger.

But before the dough rises too high, along comes the baker and *wham!* He punches it down, letting out some of the gas. Then he kneads it some more and again sets it to rise.

After a while, he may punch the bread dough down again. Then—at last—he shapes the dough into loaves.

These small loaves of dough are left to rise. When they are just the right size, the baker puts them into a large oven.

As the loaves of bread heat up, they rise more rapidly. Then, when they get very hot, they stop rising and start browning.

Soon a crisp crust forms, the bread is baked, and the baker opens the oven and takes the bread out to cool.

That's about the time that the delicious smell drifts out of the bakery door—just as the store opens!

Sometimes, if you are lucky, your mother may bake bread at home. Most of the time, however, the bread that you eat probably comes from a bakery—either a small one that you can walk past, smelling the good smell, or a huge "factory" bakery.

By adding such things as molasses, eggs, and flavorings, the

baker can make many kinds of bread and rolls.

A "factory" bakery makes bread in much the same way that a small bakery does—with one big difference. Instead of turning out a few hundred loaves of bread each day, this bakery makes thousands of loaves of bread. These loaves are wrapped in colorful paper or plastic and taken by trucks to stores all over town or even to towns far away.

If you liked this story,
read Factories *in Volume 6*
and Kitchen *in Volume 8.*

BRIDGES

Roads in the Air

If you would like to get across,
How will you get from here to there
Unless you have a magic road—
    a road built in the air?

It's fun to drive along a lake,
Especially when the weather's fair,
But you can't drive across without
    a road built in the air.

The railroad tracks can guide the train
And carry it most anywhere,
But when the way has dips, we need
    a train track in the air.

Expressways have a lot of cars.
To get across, you must take care.
It's safer if you use a walk—
    a walk built in the air.

Because of rivers, cliffs, and dips,
It's hard to get from here to there
But easy when you have a bridge—
    a bridge built in the air.

BRIDGES

Bridges That Move

All bridges are built because someone who is *here* wants to be *there*.

The castle drawbridge was built so that only friends could cross from *here* to *there*, or from *there* to *here*.

A lookout in the high tower warned when enemies were near. Then the castle folk hurried to pull one end of the bridge all the way up. Road closed! No bridge!

The idea of building bridges that could be raised or moved was so good that it is still used today.

When a tall ship approaches, the two halves of this **drawbridge** are pulled up. The cars on both sides must stop to let the ship sail through.

All drawbridges are not alike. Some rise at one end,

others turn to make way for the ship,

and some rise straight up, like an elevator.

Bridges make it easier for people—whether walking or driving or riding in trains—to get where they want to go.

If you're interested in learning about transportation, look under Automobiles *in Volume 1 and* Railroads *in Volume 13 and read* "The Water Road" *under* Canals *in Volume 3.*

BRONTE SISTERS

Three Famous Sisters

The three girls looked with excitement at the box of tiny wooden soldiers their father had brought home as a present. They couldn't wait to name each of the tiny figures. Charlotte, who was ten years old and the oldest of the three sisters, picked up one of the soldiers and said, "This shall be the Duke." Eight-year-old Emily picked up another and decided to name it "Gravey." The youngest sister, Anne, was only six. She picked out a toy soldier and named it "Waiting Boy."

Before long, Charlotte, Emily, Anne, and their brother Branwell were making up long, complicated plays about the tiny soldiers. But they soon found that they could write plays without even using the little toys. As the plays grew longer, the children decided to keep them hidden from everyone else.

Within just a few years, the sisters were writing plays in little books they made by sewing together pieces of paper. They wrote the words to their plays in such a tiny size that the books were almost impossible to read.

The Bronte children lived in England about 150 years ago, a place and time that were fun to write about. They lived in a house near a church where their father preached.

They loved to explore the moors, the wild, swampy lands between their little village of Haworth and the ocean. On the wide-open moors, the wind whipped trees and bushes into strange and fascinating shapes. Some of the stories the children wrote about took place on the moors.

The three sisters continued writing their secret plays when they were grown women. The practice they had at telling stories was enough to make all three very good writers. Together, the three sisters paid to have a book of their poems published in 1846. The book was not exactly a best-seller; only two copies were sold the year it was published.

By the very next year, however, Charlotte, Emily, and Anne had finished writing books that were popular, especially Charlotte's and Emily's. Emily's book, called *Wuthering Heights,* is about love and romance on the English moors, and is one of the most famous books ever written. Charlotte's book, called *Jane Eyre,* was a great success as soon as it was published. The three sisters, who had grown up in their own secret worlds, didn't use their real names for their first popular books. Only a year or two later did people begin to discover the real identities of the Bronte sisters.

If you like to read, you'll want to look up
Books *in Volume 2 and* Reading *in Volume 13*.

BRONTOSAUR

The Big, Big Ones

136

An animal as big as a house walked on Earth long before the first man did. Its footsteps probably made a sound like thunder. This animal was a *brontosaur,* which means "thunder lizard." It belonged to a large family of lizards called *dinosaurs*.

If there were no people on Earth when this enormous lizard lived, who named it brontosaur? The explorers who found its bones millions of years later did.

When the brontosaur lived, there were many ponds and lakes in the world. The brontosaur spent most of its time in the water. It ate only plants. Sometimes it would walk onto shore and sun itself or look for juicy leaves to eat. But it wouldn't stay long. It was so big and heavy that it got tired quickly on land. It needed the water to help support its great weight.

There was another reason why it didn't stay very long on the land. Although it was big and made a great deal of noise, it was no match for some of the fierce dinosaurs that lived on land. They weren't like the brontosaur. They didn't eat leaves. But, if they had a chance, they'd eat the brontosaur!

So if an enemy was nearby, the brontosaur would grab one more mouthful of leaves and walk slowly back into the water. It would walk deeper. And deeper. Its neck was so long that it could walk even deeper yet, all the while safely and contentedly chewing on its favorite juicy green leaves.

Did you like this story?
Read Dinosaurs *in Volume 4*
and Tyrannosaur *in Volume 15.*

BUBBLES

A Thousand Balloons in One Afternoon!

Bubbles are balloons made out of soapy water. Bubbles do not last as long as balloons made out of rubber or silk, but they are much easier to make. In just a few minutes you can make more bubbles than you can count. Here's how:

You will need one-half cup of liquid soap

a few drops of glycerin
(which your mother can buy at
the drugstore)

a thick paper straw

Pour the liquid soap into a saucer and mix in the glycerin. And that's your bubble goop!

Now it's time to make a bubble tool. Ask someone to make four small cuts near the end of your thick paper straw.

Now dip the cut part of the straw into the bubble goop.

Blow through the straw or wave it in the air. Either way you'll have lots of shining blue-green-pink-gold-silver soap bubble balloons!

Another way to make bubble balloons is to bend a thin wire into a loop at one end. Hold onto the straight end of the wire and dip the loop end into the bubble goop.

Dip it slowly and then blow gently into the middle of the soap-coated wire circle. With a little practice, you can make a big, big bubble.

BUCKINGHAM PALACE

A Famous Royal Home

When the queen of England is in London, Buckingham Palace is her home. Her family has lived there for many years.

This grand palace has more than 100 rooms. One room is the Throne Room, where the queen receives important visitors.

You could get lost in a house with so many rooms, corridors, and passages. For a long time people had a hard time just finding each other if they wanted to say something. Before telephones were put in, messengers were sent to carry notes from one room to another.

The palace is guarded by the queen's soldiers. They wear red coats and tall bearskin hats. They stand at attention by a sentry box—seeming not to move—and are not supposed to speak. When

they march in front of the palace, they are so stiff that they look like moving tin soldiers.

On certain days the queen and the people of England like to say hello to each other. People in crowds go to Buckingham Palace. They know the queen is there because her flag flies from the roof. When she is not there, the flag is taken down.

The queen and her family come out on the porch on the second floor. The people cheer and clap their hands. The queen smiles and waves to them.

*If you liked this story,
you'll like* London *in Volume 9.*

BUFFALO

King of the American Beasts

Pretend you are in the American West a long time ago when only Indians lived there.

What's that sound like faraway thunder? It isn't Indians shouting. Far across the dry and dusty plains you can see a long dark cloud touching the ground—only it isn't a cloud. You know that because of how quickly it is coming closer. Very soon you can see that it is an enormous herd of buffalo.

You have to get out of their way! You run as fast as you can to the top of a high hill. And now the huge, dark brown, shaggy animals are all around your hill on every side, galloping along to new feeding grounds.

On your high hill you wait and wait for them to pass. But the buffalo keep coming. It's a good thing you have some food and water with you because there are so many buffalo that they fill all the empty land as far as you can see. There are so many buffalo that it will take more than a whole day for them to pass!

In Africa the lion is called the king of beasts.

In America the king of beasts was once the buffalo.

The American buffalo, or *bison,* once ruled the vast prairies in great herds. In just one herd there were sometimes as many buffalo as there are people today in a city as big as Chicago.

The buffalo's head is very large. Short, thick horns curl up from either side. Long shaggy hair covers its head, humped shoulders, and front legs. It has a black beard, and its short tail ends with a tassel.

Most animals turn their backs to icy winds and flying snow.

But the buffalo faces storms head-on, just as it does bears or wolves or any other danger.

Before Columbus reached America, millions of buffalo roamed the Great Plains. But 100 years ago the buffalo had almost disappeared.

What made this happen?

Well, in the first place, buffalo had always given the Indians almost everything they needed to live. Buffalo meat supplied the Indian with his daily food. And when an Indian killed a buffalo, he could make warm clothes and moccasins, as well as walls for his tepee, from the buffalo's thick hide.

The Indians hunted buffalo with bows and arrows. They killed only enough for food and clothing.

When the white men came, everything changed. The white men brought guns, and many of them killed buffalo just for the sport of it. Still others made it a business. They killed millions of buffalo just for the hides and for buttons to be made from the horns.

Buffalo hunters were paid to kill countless more to feed the workers who were building railroads across the West. Best known of these hunters was "Buffalo Bill" Cody.

The Army also killed buffalo. In its wars with the Indians, the Army killed as many buffalo as it could to make the Indians hungry enough to surrender. Other people killed buffalo to make the Indians move away and leave their land for the many white people coming into the new country.

Because of all these things, there came a time when the millions of buffalo were gone and there were only a very few left. It seemed that soon they *all* would be gone.

Some people who loved animals became worried about this. They talked about it, and they wrote about it. The governments of Canada and the United States finally put all the buffalo they could find into national parks and other safe places.

The herds grew.

We'll probably never have millions of buffalo again, but we do have thousands. Some farmers even raise the once wild buffalo, just as they do cows and sheep.

You can see a few in almost any zoo. Or you can go west and see large herds living in much the same way as they did long ago. In Yellowstone National Park and a few other places this great shaggy creature is still king of American beasts.

Do you like learning about the American West?
Read Cowboys *in Volume 3 and* Indians *in Volume 8.*

BUGS

What Kind of Bug Is This?

If you answer, "A ladybug," you are right about its nickname. (It is also known as a ladybird beetle.) And you may know a little verse about it—

*Ladybug, ladybug,
Fly away home. . . .*

But the ladybug isn't a true bug. Not every creeping, crawling, wriggling, flying creature is a bug, as many people think. Bugs are only part of a big group of little creatures called *insects*. For example, a ladybug doesn't have thickened front wings folded over its back the way true bugs have. And it doesn't have the long, beaky mouthparts for sucking the juices of plants.

There are many different kinds of insects. They may be as tiny as a dot or as big as a mouse. They may be long or short, fat or slim, black or brightly colored. Some insects fly, some crawl, some hop.

But in some ways all full-grown insects are alike. The easiest way to know an insect is to count its legs. All insects have six legs —three pairs.

Some of these are insects.

Insects have bodies with three parts—
a head with a pair of feelers, or *antennas;*
a middle part, called *thorax,* with legs and usually wings growing from it;
a hind part, called *abdomen.*

All insects, like the dragonfly above, have a shell-like covering that they shed from time to time as they grow.

Insects have many different habits.

Bee
Makes honey

Butterfly
Flies south in late summer

Cricket
First summer concert singer

Fly
Walks upside down on the ceiling

Doodlebug
Walks backward in circles

Water Strider
Skates on the water

Mosquito
The ladies sing and sting

Cicada
Sleeps for 17 years

Firefly
Flashes a light

Mantis
Can look over its shoulder

   A caterpillar is an insect, too. It doesn't look like an insect, but it will after it turns into a butterfly. Now when you look at this picture, you know why the ant, the butterfly, the bee, and the caterpillar are insects. The earthworm isn't an insect. It doesn't have *any* legs. And the centipede has *too many* legs! Why isn't the spider an insect?

BUILDINGS

People Who Work Up High

How is it possible for these people to work up here?
It isn't . . . until the men who build skyscrapers have worked here first!

The men who build skyscrapers fit together long, heavy pieces of steel that will be the skeleton, or "bones," of a new building.

Special machines—giant cranes—lift the long pieces and hold them in place while the men fit them together.

As the building goes up, other workers do their special jobs. Some put in elevators. Others make floors, walls, or ceilings. The telephone men put in wiring and telephones. Still others put in electric wires and lights, or the pipes for bringing water to sinks, washbowls, and toilets—even to the very top floor.

Special workers put the windows in place—thousands of shining windows!

Finally, rugs and furniture are moved into the offices.

Now the building is ready for people.
Hurrying, hurrying, walking, scurrying,
 they go . . .
 across the streets,
 along the sidewalks,
 and into the tall, new building.

Up . . . up . . . up . . . up, they ride the elevators, swooping 5 . . . 10 . . . 50 floors or more above the ground.

There are some skyscrapers that go up more than 100 stories. Some builders think that someday we'll have skyscrapers more than a mile high!

A few people work on the *outside* of the finished building. Window washers keep the windows clean and bright. Climbing workers called *steeplejacks* keep towers and flagpoles painted and repaired. If there is a TV antenna on top of the building, someone makes sure that its lights stay lit at night so that airplanes won't bump into it.

*To learn about people who live up high,
read* "Going Up" *under* Homes *in Volume 7.*

BUNYAN, PAUL

A Very Special Lumberjack

If somebody told you that a giant had cut down all the trees between the Atlantic Ocean and the Rocky Mountains, would you believe it? Maybe if you tried hard enough you might *almost* believe it. It might be fun to pretend to believe it.

Stories like that are called *tall stories*. A lot of tall stories are told about a lumberjack named Paul Bunyan. (A *lumberjack* is a man who earns his living by cutting down big trees in a forest so that we can have wood for building houses and making furniture.)

Paul Bunyan was a very special lumberjack. According to the stories, he was so big that when he sneezed, a whole hillside of pine trees would fall over. Then he might pick up one of the fallen trees and use it to comb out his long, black beard!

You can imagine that being so big, Paul would get very hungry. He especially liked pancakes—or *flapjacks,* as the lumberjacks called them. The frying pan that Paul's flapjacks were made in was so big that several men would skate around in it with slabs of bacon tied to their feet. This greased the pan so that the flapjacks wouldn't stick.

One reason that Paul could cut down so many trees and haul them away was that he had a famous helper. He found his helper during the "blue winter." People called it the "blue winter" because the snow fell and fell that year, and it was all blue snow! Maybe the snow was blue because it was so very cold. Anyway, one night Paul heard something crying. When he went to look, he found a pair of silky blue ears sticking out of the snow. Paul pulled and pulled, and out of the blue snow came a small baby blue ox that had lost its mother!

Paul took the little blue ox home with him and named it Babe. When Babe grew up, he was nearly as big as a small mountain.

Once in Wisconsin, by the Mississippi River, the lumberjacks found a log road that had so many curves in it that they didn't know whether they were coming or going. Paul laughed, and the townspeople ran into their houses when they felt the great wind and heard the roaring sound of Paul's laugh.

He picked up one end of the road and tied it to Babe, who tugged and pulled all the curves out of the road. People in the north woods say you can tell for sure that the story is true because today you can still see that road running straight through the woods without turning.

You may read about a famous pioneer who told tall stories under Davy Crockett *in Volume 3.*

BUTTONS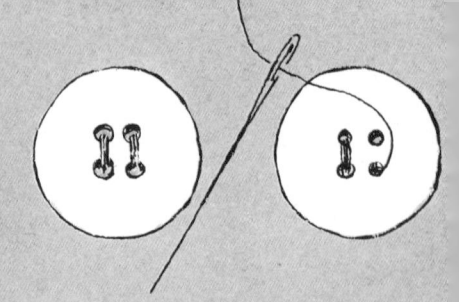

Holding Clothes Together

"What shall I take to school today for show-and-tell?" Max was wondering while he dressed. His mother brought him his red-and-white-checked shirt. But when he put it on, he saw that a button was gone.

"We'll find you another shirt," his mother said.

"But I want to wear this one," Max said.

"Oh, dear," his mother said.

"I can pin it shut."

"That wouldn't look very good," his mother said. "Buttons are for keeping clothes fastened together. We'll have to find you another button."

Max's mother went to get the button box. She and Max looked in it for a button like those on his shirt. There were purple buttons, black buttons, and red buttons. There were buttons as round as marbles, and there were square buttons. But Max and his mother were looking for a white button as flat as a penny and about as big around as the end of Max's thumb.

While they were searching, Max asked, "Why don't people tape their shirts shut or buckle them shut?"

"Because buttons are easier," his mother answered.

"Did people always use buttons to keep their clothes shut?"

"I don't know," his mother answered. But she promised that she would look it up in the encyclopedia and tell him when he got home from school.

Just then they found the button that they were looking for. Max's mother threaded a needle and sewed on the button.

Max put on his shirt. He and his mother jumped into the car and drove to school. They got there just in time. As he got out of the car, the bell was ringing.

"Oh," he said, "I forgot to bring something for show-and-tell time!"

That night when he came home from school, his mother asked, "Didn't I hear someone ask me about buttons this morning?"

"*I* asked you," Max answered.

So his mother told him how buttons got started. "Four thousand years ago," she said, "Chinese people wore buttons just because they were pretty. They cost too much to use for holding clothes together. A very important Chinese man might have just one gold button sewed on his cap. Buckles and pins and string were used to hold clothes together.

"When people did start to use buttons to hold clothes together, their buttons were made of wood or nuts or seashells or bone or brass or iron or ivory. Now most buttons, like the ones on your shirt, are made of plastic, just as your toy soldiers are."

"I didn't know all that," Max said.

His mother laughed. "Buttons are so little you just forget they're there until you lose one."

Max laughed, too, because he had just thought of something. "I know," he said, "I'll take our button box for the next show-and-tell at school!"

At one time, shoes were fastened with buttons instead of strings. The buttons were so hard to handle that people used a special *buttonhook* to pull them through the holes.

Buttons aren't used so much now as they used to be. Do you know why? Somebody invented *zippers*.

Some people collect buttons. They try to see how many different kinds of buttons they can find for their collections.

Credits

Pages	Art	Text
6-13	Perl	Fadiman, Johnson
14-19	Fraser	Johnson
20-21	Aronson	Postma
22-27	Sherwood	Dennis
28-29	Stine	Dennis
30-35	Masheris	Johnson
36-39	Kane	Johnson
40-43	Kane	Zucker
44-49	Keely	Nims
50-51	Stine	Klinger
52-53	Stine	Postma
54-55	Stine	F. Gies
56-59	Suyeoka	Dennis
60-63	O'Sullivan	Nims
64-65	Keane	Dennis
66-69	Ruth	Zucker
70-73	Wills	Bjorck
74-79	Murakami	Zucker
80-85	Chapman	Johnson
86-87	Aronson	Lerner
88-89	Aronson	Zucker
90-91	Kane	Dennis
92-95	Suyeoka	Dennis
96-99	Fraser	Johnson
100-101	Perl	Nims
102-107	Stine	Zucker
108-111	Taylor	Nims
112-113	Taylor	Walker
114-115	Madden	Dennis
116-117	Walworth	Fadiman
118-119	Fredericks	Dennis
120-121	Stine	Lerner
122-125	Stine	Stevenson
126-127	Oechsli	Dennis
128-131	Armstrong	Klinger
132-133	Burke	Dennis
134-135	Aronson	Lerner
136-137	Murakami	Klinger
138-139	Oechsli	Nims
140-141	Gallagher	Riggan
142-145	Mitchell	L. Reeve
146-149	Walworth	Bjorck
150-153	Fredericks	Johnson
154-155	Taylor	Dupee
156-159	Oechsli	Walker